ISBN 0-7398-8810-2

12   2331   18

4500704942

Rigby • Steck-Vaughn

www.HarcourtAchieve.com

1.800.531.5015

Contents

FUNCTIONAL READING COMPREHENSION

Skill Focus Lessons

PRACTICE POSTTEST FOR STANFORD 10
Test Battery, Advanced 1 Level

Reading Vocabulary

Choose the word or group of words that means the same, or about the same, as the underlined word. Then mark the space for the answer you have chosen.

SAMPLE A

Something that is broad is —

A near

B wide

C hard

D empty

3

Someone who is prominent is —

A honest

B hardy

C progressive

D notable

1

To acknowledge is to —

A attempt

B admit

C explain

D refuse

4

To heave something is to —

A hurl

B improvise

C depart

D hit

2

A tariff is a —

A contest

B pamphlet

C tax

D law

5

Gaunt refers to someone's —

A reactions

B feelings

C attitude

D appearance

6

A ballad is a —

A vote   **C** song

B list   **D** party

7

Something that is barren is —

A brutal   **C** empty

B changeable   **D** durable

8

To dwell is to —

A draft   **C** recite

B live   **D** move

9

If something is basted, it is —

A moistened   **C** bartered

B governed   **D** replaced

10

A mallet is a —

A clan   **C** hammer

B duty   **D** pageant

11

Something that is tedious is —

A repetitive   **C** sullen

B radiant   **D** tiresome

12

Something that is ebony is —

A blue   **C** beige

B black   **D** gray

DIRECTIONS ▶

Read the sentence in the box. Then choose the answer in which the underlined word is used in the same way. Mark the space for the answer you have chosen.

SAMPLE B

> Jillian's walking pace is faster this year.

In which sentence does the word pace mean the same as in the sentence above?

A Lin has increased her racing pace this month.

B A builder may pace off the length of the foundation.

C When she is nervous, she will often pace the room.

D Pace yourself during your run.

13

> Some people weigh themselves daily when they diet.

In which sentence does the word weigh mean the same as in the sentence above?

A Shoppers weigh fruit to figure out the cost.

B Judges must weigh their words when they speak.

C Making the right choice will weigh on my mind.

D Wrestlers weigh in before competing.

14

> We walked near the park today.

In which sentence does the word near mean the same as in the sentence above?

A Basketball season is drawing near.

B Her near win in the election made her supporters happy.

C As we near home, we hear the dog.

D Near the football field is the pool.

15

> Mrs. Sanchez put a label on each jar of vegetables.

In which sentence does the word label mean the same as in the sentence above?

A It is rare to see that fashion designer's label on shirts.

B My favorite singer changed to a new record label.

C Write a label that describes each item on the sale table.

D Label each bone on the drawing of the skeleton.

16

How many books can you jam into a locker?

In which sentence does the word jam mean the same as in the sentence above?

A Be careful not to jam your finger closing the window.

B The secretary fixed the paper jam in the copier.

C You cannot jam one more sock in that drawer!

D Mr. Wilson was stuck in a traffic jam.

17

Was the object in the canoe's path a log?

In which sentence does the word object mean the same as in the sentence above?

A Can you find the object of the verb in that sentence?

B What was the object of his yelling?

C The coach may object to that ruling.

D The object in the roadway was too dark to see.

18

Please make sure the children are quiet before the movie begins.

In which sentence does the word quiet mean the same as in the sentence above?

A During study hall the library is usually quiet.

B Please ask the painter to quiet down the color.

C I'm not going to the game; I want a quiet evening at home.

D The ringing of the bell will quiet the class.

19

Every spring our class has a sports day ending with a race.

In which sentence does the word race mean the same as in the sentence above?

A Our whole class will be in the three-legged race.

B The two candidates are in a close race for class president.

C I watched my cat Tabby try to race up the tree.

D George Washington Carver was an honored member of the black race.

20

The bag of cement was too heavy to move.

In which sentence does the word bag mean the same as in the sentence above?

A My brother's job is to bag groceries at the market.

B My brother carried a bag of groceries into the house.

C My sister usually carries a shoulder bag, not a backpack.

D Those pants are too large for him; they will bag.

21

The safe was empty; the money was gone.

In which sentence does the word safe mean the same as in the sentence above?

A The animals caught in the storm were safe.

B I try to keep my homework safe from the dog.

C My grandfather keeps his will in a safe.

D The runner was safe at home plate.

DIRECTIONS ▶

As you read each sentence, use the other words in the sentence to help you figure out what the underlined word means. Then mark the space for the answer you have chosen.

SAMPLE C

The comedian wore a <u>bizarre</u> costume made from rags. <u>Bizarre</u> means —

A colorful

B plain

C neat

D odd

23

The rebels raised a <u>bulwark</u> to keep the soldiers out. <u>Bulwark</u> means —

A fuss

B blockade

C riot

D reward

22

Hank gazed at me <u>acidly</u> when he saw I had damaged his bicycle. <u>Acidly</u> means —

A sharply

B carefully

C casually

D briefly

24

<u>Pandemonium</u> broke out when the fight began. <u>Pandemonium</u> means —

A peace

B confusion

C opposition

D interest

25

The <u>fastidious</u> dresser would never use a safety pin for a button. <u>Fastidious</u> means —

A elaborate   **C** fussy

B happy   **D** unknown

26

Mariah made the <u>ludicrous</u> statement that pigs have wings. <u>Ludicrous</u> means —

A absurd   **C** believable

B polite   **D** hostile

27

As we sat around the campfire, Peter told the story of a lengthy <u>skirmish</u> in the war. <u>Skirmish</u> means —

A lie   **C** battle

B skyscraper   **D** specimen

28

Use <u>tact</u> when you speak to the teacher about your problem with the assignment. <u>Tact</u> means —

A sincerity   **C** ingenuity

B politeness   **D** humor

29

Does the sun <u>radiate</u> heat to Earth? <u>Radiate</u> means —

A rush   **C** reduce

B raise   **D** send

30

That boy has <u>slovenly</u> habits; his room looks like a pigsty. <u>Slovenly</u> means —

A messy   **C** neat

B elaborate   **D** friendly

Reading Comprehension

DIRECTIONS ▶

Read each passage. Then read each question about the passage. Decide which is the best answer to the question. Mark the space for the answer you have chosen.

SAMPLES

The Harvest Moon

The harvest moon is the full moon that occurs each year closest to the first day of autumn. For centuries people have thought that this moon looked bigger and brighter than any other moon, and for centuries people have held celebrations to honor it. The harvest moon is not really bigger or brighter than any other moon, but it looks like it is because it is closer to the horizon. At this time of year the moon travels on its lowest path. For several days in a row, it appears close to the horizon just as the sun sets. On clear autumn nights the moon glows brilliantly. Some people think it looks orange.

In agricultural communities long ago, farmers took advantage of the bright light of this autumn moon to harvest their crops. Many people in these communities believed that the harvest moon appeared in the sky to signal the end of the harvest. Many others believed it appeared to grant them successful crops. People all over the world held lavish festivals under the harvest moon. China, for example, still holds a harvest moon festival. The celebration in China involves telling stories of Heng O, a figure in Chinese myths who controlled the fruitfulness of the harvest. The people of China honor the moon by baking round cakes and stamping them with an image of Heng O. Then they take these cakes to the festival and exchange them with friends and relatives to wish them happiness and luck with the next year's crops.

A The harvest moon festival in China is *mainly* a celebration of —

A the holidays

B the harvest

C Heng O

D the full moon

B Which of the following is true of the autumn moon?

A It grants successful crops.

B It houses Heng O.

C It controls the earth's fruitfulness.

D It travels near the horizon.

Winter Necklace

Hurrying home from school,

my breath forming clouds before my face,

I stop to stare at a row of black birds

huddled on a wire over the street.

5 Too numerous to count,

too still to seem capable of flight,

they hang above me like beads

on an endless black necklace.

Falling from a nearby eave, an icicle

10 shatters on pavement.

A sharp crack startles the air.

As if a necklace string has snapped,

the birds spill and clatter

into the gray, felt sky.

1

Which of the following events causes the primary action in the poem?

A The speaker walks home from school.

B Birds huddle on a wire above the street.

C An icicle falls from a nearby eave.

D Birds rise and fly into the air.

2

What is the main idea of this poem?

A Warmer weather is preferable to colder weather.

B Stillness and activity can have surprising contrasts.

C Noise pollution in cities is harmful to animals.

D Birds and humans share numerous similarities.

3

A "gray, felt sky" suggests what sort of weather conditions?

A Blizzard   **C** Cloudy

B Clear   **D** Rainy

4

Line 2 describes "breath forming clouds before my face." The use of *b* and *f* sounds is an example of what literary device?

A Alliteration   **C** Antithesis

B Allusion   **D** Assonance

5

Why does the speaker stop to stare at the birds?

A Fascination   **C** Disgust

B Boredom   **D** Sadness

6

Why does the poem say the birds "spill and clatter" into the air?

A To emphasize the sudden noisiness of their flight

B To strengthen the comparison between birds and beads

C To show that the birds are creating a messy situation

D To highlight the speaker's reaction to the birds' flight

All Flows Lead to the Sea

Imagine standing on a rocky outcropping thirty or forty feet above a sparkling lake of clear blue water. You watch children playing at the water's edge with balls and boxes, anything they can find in their village that has been discarded. One child begins putting things into the lake to see what happens, and everything she tosses in the water floats. Then the children themselves leap into the water, moving deeper and deeper until you are certain they can no longer touch the bottom. Yet, there they are floating in the lake, as if their legs have stretched forty feet to the bottom. On this day, at this time, as you watch these playful children, the Dead Sea seems very much alive.

The Dead Sea sits in the Great Rift Valley, between the countries of Israel and Jordan. Much of its fifty miles in length forms part of the border between the two countries, but the countries do not fight over who owns this body of water. Why is it called the Dead Sea? It is called the Dead Sea because almost nothing can live in its waters, except for a few types of plants and one type of inedible shrimp. The water in the Dead Sea is nine times as salty as ocean water. Drinking the water from the Dead Sea would be like dumping an entire box of salt into a glass, pouring water on top of it, and drinking it.

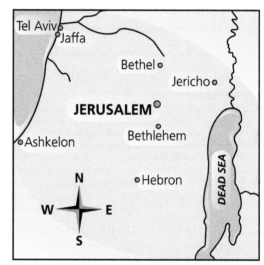

Nevertheless, a few positive things can be said about the Dead Sea. At 1,310 feet below sea level, it is the lowest place on Earth. Because it is so low, water from rivers and streams flows into the Dead Sea, but nothing ever flows out. This means that when the water evaporates in the extreme heat of this region, salt and other minerals are left behind. The Dead Sea Works, a mineral company, takes these minerals from the Dead Sea and sells them to make salt much like that which you put on your food.

The Dead Sea is also good for tourism. Every year thousands and thousands of people want to come to the Great Rift Valley to tell their friends that they have stood at the lowest point on Earth. They do not come just to stand, however. They also come to float in the waters of the Dead Sea. Tourists are always amazed that they can float in water that is only a few inches deep! The high concentration of minerals keeps the human body popping up to the top. Just be sure not to take a drink.

7

What keeps water from flowing out of the Dead Sea?

A The water sits far below sea level.

B The Dead Sea has several dams.

C Salt keeps the water from moving.

D The water evaporates too quickly.

8

This passage is *mainly* about —

A how Earth's geography makes the Dead Sea so salty

B how mineral companies use the salt from the Dead Sea

C how some parts of the Dead Sea are useful

D how some parts of the Dead Sea are fun for tourists

9

Which would be true about most very salty bodies of water?

A They would connect to an ocean.

B They would lie in an area with very hot temperatures.

C Few people would swim in them.

D Few plants and animals live there.

10

What information would help the reader figure out the percentage of salt in the Dead Sea?

A How many plants are in the sea

B The percentage of salt in the ocean

C The percentage of salt in tap water

D How many people float in the sea

11

To understand if people can float in the Dead Sea, you should ask —

A why salt in water makes things float

B how deep the Dead Sea is

C why saltwater does not taste good

D how minerals are taken from the sea

12

Why does the author explain why nothing lives in the Dead Sea just before telling about the Dead Sea Works?

A To introduce unusual shrimp

B To tell how salt is beneficial

C To describe the Dead Sea Works

D To explain that Jordan does not use minerals

Dear Readers,

Wow! The staff of *World of Pets* knew you would enjoy our contest to choose a picture of an interesting pet for the cover of our next issue. We didn't know how *much* you would enjoy it, though. You surprised us by sending in more than 4,000 entries! Your tremendous response has made this contest our most popular ever.

You sent us photographs, videos, posters, and even sculptures of all kinds of pets, from dogs and cats to lizards and canaries. Your contest-entry essays included funny and heartwarming stories. Some of you included newspaper articles about silly pet tricks or rescues made by animals. Your entries reminded us why pets are such a vital part of our lives and why we love them so much.

The picture of our contest winner will appear on the cover of next month's issue. The winner and two runners-up will be featured in the lead article. You won't want to miss this special issue!

Thanks for all of your fascinating entries about many truly outstanding animals. We hope you had as much fun completing your pet-contest entries as we had reviewing them.

Sincerely,

Selena Garcia

Selena Garcia,
Editor-in-Chief, *World of Pets*

13

Which words from the letter *best* show the variety of animals that readers entered in the contest?

A "all kinds of pets"

B "sending in more than 4,000 entries"

C "from dogs and cats to lizards and canaries"

D "photographs, videos, posters, and even sculptures"

14

Based on the letter, which of the following was probably required to enter the contest?

A Making a video of a pet

B Drawing a cartoon of a pet

C Writing an essay about a pet

D Making a video of a silly pet trick

15

You can assume that readers of *World of Pets* probably —

A have many interests

B have more than one pet

C are friends of pet owners

D are enthusiastic pet owners

16

What words give the letter a personal and friendly tone?

A "we" and "our"

B "you" and "your"

C "funny and heartwarming stories"

D "silly pet tricks ... made by animals"

17

Readers who did *not* enter the contest probably would —

A scan the letter for details about current events

B skim the letter for interesting information

C read the letter carefully to learn something about the contest

D take notes on the letter in order to record important information

18

The next issue of *World of Pets* probably will be —

A devoted to unusual pets

B longer than a typical issue

C popular with contest entrants

D devoted to pets from other lands

A Hard Worker

"What are you looking at, Grandpa?" Audra asked, taking a seat across from him at his desk. He looked up and directed his smile toward her.

"Take a look," he said, and pushed the object in her direction.

The object was a picture frame. Inside it was a tattered black-and-white picture of a man in overalls. The overalls were stained with mud, and so were the man's face and hands. One hand held the handle of a heavy-looking hammer almost as long as the man's leg. The man's back was somewhat bent, but his smile was broad.

"That's my father," said Grandpa.

"Why is he so dirty?" asked Audra.

"He was a foreman on a railroad," said Grandpa. "He helped lay the tracks that trains run on today. This picture was taken back when cameras were still pretty new."

Audra studied the man's kind face, his gnarled hands. "Why is he bent over like that?" she asked. "Is it from pounding those metal spikes?"

"Pounding spikes wasn't easy," agreed Grandpa, "but my father suffered from arthritis. His back was almost always in pain. He was bent over like that for his entire adult life."

Audra was amazed. "Why didn't he find an easier job?"

"Back then, jobs were scarce," said Grandpa. "My dad was also a farmer, but the railroad paid better. When he got this job, he asked me to take over the family farm."

"How long did he work on the railroad?"

"He did it for a long time. He helped lay track over and sometimes even through mountains. He rode the train miles to work every morning, and the train brought him all the way back every evening. He worked until the railroad had all the track it needed, and then he was out of a job."

"That's not fair!" said Audra, who felt a *surge* of anger at her great-grandfather's misfortune. "He deserved better treatment."

"I thought so, too," said Grandpa, "but my father never complained. He taught me to be grateful for what I have and to work hard every day. It's a lesson I never forgot."

Audra was quiet as a rabbit for a long moment. Then she asked, "What are you planning to do this afternoon?"

"It's such a nice day," said Grandpa, "I thought I might work in the garden."

"Would you like some help?" she asked.

"I would love some," he replied, smiling.

19

If you didn't know the meaning of the word *surge*, the words around it would tell you it means what?

A Doubt

C Increase

B Image

D Odor

20

Which detail from the picture shows that Grandpa's father was a hard worker?

A He held a hammer.

B He was smiling.

C He was covered in mud.

D He wore overalls.

21

Why is Audra "quiet as a rabbit for a long moment"?

A She can't think of anything more to say about her great-grandfather.

B She's thinking about times she's complained about hard work.

C She's hungry and thinking about what to eat for lunch.

D She's remembering the last time she rode a train.

22

What is an important method of storytelling in this passage?

A Diary

C Dialect

B Dialogue

D Diagram

23

Which fact about his father does Grandpa value most?

A He laid track over and through mountains.

B He suffered from arthritis for his entire adult life.

C He asked Grandpa to take over the family farm.

D He never complained about his misfortunes.

24

After learning about her great-grandfather, Audra offers to help in the garden because she —

A is inspired by the story of his life

B hopes to avoid a more difficult chore

C feels sorry for her grandfather

D wants to get some exercise

The Forgotten Pilot

Many people of a certain age can tell you exactly where they were and what they were doing during some of the most incredible moments in history. For example, when Neil Armstrong and Buzz Aldrin became the first human beings to land on the moon, most people were probably glued to their television sets. Then Neil Armstrong, the mission's commander, said one of the most famous phrases in American history. "That's one small step for a man, one giant leap for mankind." The grainy images actually showed the two astronauts setting foot on the moon.

One person who did not hear Armstrong's famous words or see the video footage of his landing on the moon was Michael Collins. As strange as it seems, Collins was only a few hundred miles away when it happened. How can that be? The moon is more than 200,000 miles away from Earth. Michael Collins was not on Earth at the time. Instead, he was a few hundred miles above Armstrong and Aldrin, piloting the command module, *Columbia*. The astronauts needed this spacecraft to get them back to Earth once they had completed their mission. Many people remember Neil Armstrong and Buzz Aldrin, but what about Michael Collins, the forgotten pilot?

Born in Italy, Collins went to high school in our nation's capital, Washington, D.C. Wanting to be a pilot, Collins went to college at the U.S. Military Academy. Upon graduation, he joined the Air Force and became a test pilot for some of the fastest planes the world had ever seen. Sometimes Collins would be the first to fly in a new type of plane. It was his job to test the plane and make sure it worked. If it didn't, it was then Collins's job to figure out a way to land it without destroying the plane, or himself.

It was a dangerous job, but Collins seemed to like being the first to do things. In 1963, he became one of the first astronauts. In 1966, he piloted the Gemini spacecraft as it docked with two different unoccupied spacecraft on the same mission. Due to his skill in piloting that Gemini mission, Collins was chosen to pilot the first flight to the moon. Even though he was not one of the astronauts to walk on the moon for the first time, Collins seemed to appreciate what was happening. He later said, "I think a future flight should include a poet, a priest, and a philosopher . . . we might get a much better idea of what we saw."

25

After graduating from college, Michael Collins joined the —

A Army   **C** Navy

B Marines   **D** Air Force

26

Which of the following supports the idea that Collins was in awe of going to the moon?

A The quotation at the end of the passage

B The quotation at the beginning of the passage

C His fear of becoming an astronaut

D His sadness at having to stay in the ship

27

What information is included in most biographical passages?

A Information on the subject's friends

B The place where the subject was born

C Why the subject has been forgotten

D Where the subject was during a historic event

28

With which statement would the author of this passage *most likely* agree?

A Too many people become astronauts.

B Michael Collins should be more famous.

C Not enough people saw the first moon landing.

D Michael Collins should be a mission commander.

29

After reading the title of the passage and the end of the first two paragraphs, the reader should —

A read the title again

B read the sentence again

C read the first paragraph again

D read the quote from Armstrong again

30

Which does the author include?

A The name of Collins's spacecraft

B The name of Armstrong's spacecraft

C The name of the moon landing mission

D The name of the experiments

Software Solutions Catalog 24

Fun and Games

Our Most Popular Computer Game!

Award Winner!

Undersea Nation!®

Take control as you build your own world from the ocean floor up! The computer game Undersea Nation!® uses real graphics and sound effects to bring you face to face with dozens of amazing deep-sea adventures. What kind of underwater world will you create? You decide who lives in your nation, where they work, what they do for fun, and how they can respond if something goes wrong. Introduce more fantasy with imaginary sea creatures or make the kingdom seem real with sunken ships and sharks. Undersea Nation!® includes over 80 underwater challenges, complete sound effects, and rocking great music. *This is your chance to own a truly outstanding computer game!*

Ages 8–Up
Computer Requirements:
64 MB processor, 300 MB free HD space,
16 MB 3D video card, TrueSound® compatible
sound card; works with all computer platforms.

Was $19.95

Now Only **$12.95**

- Problem Solving
- Demonstrating Creativity
- Using Math Skills
- Developing Knowledge of Science

SAVE
$7.00!

31

Catalog readers interested in oceans and in computer games probably would —

A read the description carefully

B skim or skip over the description

C take notes on the description

D scan the description for details about other computer games

34

Which words from the description tell about a fact?

A "rocking great music"

B "amazing deep-sea adventures"

C "over 80 underwater challenges"

D "a truly outstanding computer game."

32

The catalog designer probably uses italic type to —

A save time

B help inform the reader

C appeal to a wide audience

D direct the reader's attention

35

The makers of Undersea Nation!® probably believe that computer-game players enjoy —

A improving their computer skills

B solving complex math puzzles

C studying types of marine life

D imagining themselves controlling people and events

33

Most people who play Undersea Nation!® will —

A create stories for new games

B make decisions and solve problems

C be discouraged by its challenges

D learn about the history of the world's oceans

36

Based on the description in this ad, makers of computer games probably try to make their games —

A realistic

C humorous

B exciting

D frightening

The Chickasaw and Choctaw Nations

Long ago a great people—a small group, but brave—lived in a desolate land in the far west. One day their god, Ababinili, visited the elders and the holy men and told them to search for a better home in the bright domain toward the rising sun. The elders and holy men delivered Ababinili's message to the people, and the people began to prepare for the journey.

The travels of these people were guided by a sacred staff, or walking stick. At the end of each day's journey, the staff was stuck into the ground by the holy man carrying it. During the night, Ababinili moved the staff so that it pointed in the direction he wanted the people to go—almost always toward the sunrise.

The people had many adventures on their journey. At one point they were blocked by a flood, so they built rafts in order to cross the waters. Later, a raven delivered a gift of corn from Ababinili to be planted when they reached their new home. Soon after the people had crossed the greatest river in the land, they awoke one morning to find that the staff had not moved in the night. They had reached their new home.

Two leaders, named Chacta and Chicsa, could not agree, however, on which area of land would make the better home. Eventually, they decided that the people should split into two groups and settle in adjacent territories. The larger group became known as the Choctaw, and its cousin group became known as the Chickasaw.

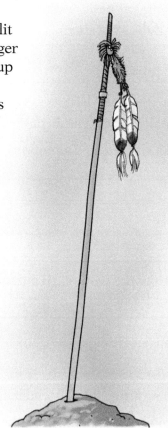

The two groups lived near the great river as neighbors for countless seasons, until the arrival of settlers from across the ocean. Battles were fought with these new neighbors, but the bravery of the Chickasaw and Choctaw could not overcome the numbers against them. Once again the people packed up to move, but this time it was not the will of Ababinili, but that of the settlers driving them back toward the desolate lands of the west.

Even in the midst of this sorrow, when death walked among them, the people stood by one another. Although they now called themselves by different names, the two groups had not forgotten their common bond. Shelter, food, and fellowship were shared until all the people had settled into their new home. Even today, the people have not forgotten, and the story of the Chickasaw is not complete unless it includes the Choctaw, too.

37

The author of this passage —

A expresses sadness about the historical treatment of the groups

B does not believe the story of the origin of the groups is based in fact

C thinks the Chickasaw and Choctaw Nations should reunite

D appreciates the revival of history and culture the two groups enjoy

38

How did the people find their way to their new home?

A They followed a raft downstream.

B A raven flew overhead.

C The holy men guided them.

D A staff pointed the way.

39

Which of the following *best* summarizes this passage?

A The groups are very brave.

B The groups are interesting.

C The groups have suffered greatly.

D The groups are like other groups.

40

What reveals the *most* about the Chickasaw and Choctaw Nations?

A Chacta and Chicsa could not agree on where to make a good home.

B Long ago a great people lived in a desolate land in the far west.

C The story of the Chickasaw must include the Choctaw, too.

D Chacta and Chicsa decided that the people should split up.

41

What importance do the raft and the raven have in the passage?

A To demonstrate resourcefulness

B To provide a timeline for the events

C To show that the journey was long

D To show that the journey was wet

42

Which way does Ababinili want the people to go?

A East   **C** South

B North   **D** West

The Didgeridoo

One of the most remarkable musical instruments in the world is the didgeridoo. This ancient instrument, with an unusual sounding name, is actually one of the oldest instruments in the world.

The didgeridoo is an instrument used by the Aborigine people of Australia. It is really a very simple-looking instrument, but there is nothing simple about learning to play it. Most didgeridoos are long, hollowed-out pieces of wood or bamboo. The easiest way to make one is to get a piece of wood from a tree that has been attacked by termites. Most didgeridoos measure 4 to 5 feet long, but some can be over 10 feet in length. This difference in length can make a difference in the sound of the instrument.

People who study musical instruments classify the didgeridoo as a woodwind. A person plays the didgeridoo by blowing air through the instrument. However, if you just put your lips to the opening and blow, you will not make the sound you want. The didgeridoo uses vibrations to make its sounds. To cause vibrations, the musician needs to make his or her lips vibrate while blowing air into the instrument. It is this vibration, combined with the moving air, that causes the didgeridoo to make its sound. Musicians use this process to play oboes and saxophones, except that oboes and saxophones have small pieces of wood called reeds in their mouthpieces. These reeds vibrate to produce sound in the instrument.

To make more than one sound at a time in the didgeridoo, the musician practices something called *circular breathing*. This means that at the same time the musician is blowing air into the didgeridoo, he or she is also breathing air in. Have you ever tried to speak and breathe at the same time? The key to circular breathing is to gather air into your cheeks, then blow it into the instrument very gradually. As you are blowing gradually, you breathe air in gradually as well. As the air comes into your lungs, you move it from your lungs to your cheeks and start the process all over again.

The Aborigines often play for very long periods of time because, they say, "If the earth had a voice, it would be the sound of the didgeridoo."

43

To get a sound from a didgeridoo, a person should first —

A practice circular breathing

B insert a reed into the opening

C begin vibrating his or her lips

D blow hard into the small opening

44

From this passage, the reader can conclude that —

A most didgeridoos are bamboo

B oboes and didgeridoos are similar in length

C saxophone players practice circular breathing

D a person cannot speak and breathe at the same time

45

How can this passage be classified?

A An evaluation of an art

B An explanation of how to do something

C A description of a native people

D The history of an unusual instrument

46

Which detail about didgeridoos is *not* included in the text?

A When the first didgeridoo was made

B How to make a didgeridoo

C Where the first didgeridoo came from

D The type of instrument a didgeridoo is

47

Which supports the idea that people playing the oboe do not need to make their lips vibrate?

A Oboes are woodwinds.

B Oboes are 4 feet in length.

C Oboes use a reed that vibrates.

D Oboes are similar to saxophones.

48

Based on the passage, which is true of most musical instruments?

A Longer instruments can be played for longer periods of time.

B Instruments that are simple to make are difficult to play.

C Circular breathing helps musicians.

D Instruments that use air and are made of wood are called woodwinds.

Playing with Clay

A Clay Jar with a Lid

Need a special container to store small treasures? Why not make one yourself? Follow these simple directions to create your own ceramic jar. Don't forget to decorate it in your favorite style and colors.

What You Need:
- ✔ self-hardening clay
- ✔ fork
- ✔ Knife
- ✔ paint brush
- ✔ rolling pin
- ✔ ruler
- ✔ jar lid
- ✔ decorating supplies (optional)

What You Do:

1. Use a rolling pin to flatten a ball of clay to about an eighth of an inch thick.

2. Use a jar lid as a guide to cut out two circles of clay. One circle will form the bottom of the jar; the other will be the lid. Then cut a large slab of clay big enough to wrap around the two clay circles to become the sides of the jar.

3. Use a fork to score the edges of one of the circles and all but one of the long edges of the slab. These score marks will show where to attach pieces to each other.

4. With a brush, moisten all the scored edges with water. Wrap the slab into a tube and press the scored, moist edges together. Attach the other scored edge of the tube to the scoring on the clay circle.

5. Cut out a shape for the lid handle and attach the handle to the remaining clay circle. Attach a coil of clay far enough inside the circle to keep the lid in place on your jar.

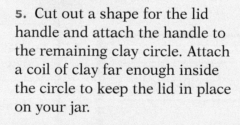

After your jar and lid have dried, decorate them with paint, glitter, yarn, or anything you want to apply with glue!

49

Which necessary ingredient is *not* listed in the instructions?

A Jar lid

B Water

C Rolling pin

D Self-hardening clay

50

Written instructions for a project should have —

A a figure of speech

B a series of steps

C questions and answers

D complex sentences and paragraphs

51

People who enjoy this project probably —

A are good artists

B do not play sports

C like to make things

D cannot afford to spend much money

52

Which information is shown in an illustration?

A When to paint the jar

B How much clay to use

C How to handle the fork

D Where to moisten the clay

53

According to the instructions, which of the following steps are *not* in the correct order?

A Roll out the clay; cut out the shapes

B Cut out the shapes; score the edges

C Gather the materials; roll out the clay

D Paint the pieces; assemble the pieces

54

A "What You Need" list could *best* be used to —

A write a story

B make friends

C shop for a bicycle

D go on a camping trip

Reading Vocabulary

Recognizing Synonyms

With over 800,000 words in the English Language, it's not surprising that some words mean much the same thing as other words. *Synonyms* are words with similar meanings. You can use synonyms in a number of situations. For example, to perform research on the internet or in the library, substitute a synonym for your search term to help you broaden your search and find information. Synonyms also help you in your writing. Effective authors choose synonyms to avoid repeating the same word and making their writing dull. Synonyms help to make their writing more precise and vivid.

Here are some strategies to determine the best synonym for a given word.

HINT

If you can answer this question, you should be able to think of a synonym: What is the intended meaning?

1. Read the item, paying close attention to the underlined word.

2. Read all of the answer choices before selecting an answer.

3. Make up an example sentence useing the underlined word.

4. Try each of your answer choices in place of the underlined word in the example sentence. Does the answer choice fit in the sentence without changing the meaning?

5. Then, narrow your choices by eliminating answers that you believe are incorrect.

Determining Correct Choices Suppose you are asked to name a synonym for the word congratulate. What word might be a good synonym for congratulate? Here are four possible choices:

Does thank mean the same as congratulate?

Does praise mean the same as congratulate?

Does admire mean the same as congratulate?

Does consider mean the same as congratulate?

How could you go about determining the correct answer?

You could write a sentence using the word congratulate. An example sentence may be something like "The teacher will congratulate the winner of the spelling bee."

Try the first choice in the sentence. Thank can be eliminated because it doesn't make sense in the sentence.

- Be aware of choices that seem close in meaning but are not the best synonym for the word. Admire can be eliminated because even though it might fit, it is not the best synonym for the word.

- Be aware of choices that sound somewhat similar to the word in the item. In this example, consider sounds a bit similar to congratulate, but these two words do not mean the same thing. Consider is not a synonym for congratulate.

- Study the sentence you create for clues to the correct meaning of the word. In the above example, the word winner suggests that something positive like the word praise. Therefore, the best synonym for congratulate is praise.

An Extra Example Here's another example. Suppose you are asked to name a synonym for the word support. What word might be a good synonym for support? Here are four possible choices:

Does withstand mean the same as support?

Does suppose mean the same as support?

Does consider mean the same as support?

Does approve mean the same as support?

How could you go about determining the correct answer?

You could write a sentence that uses the word support. For example, "The people will support the plan for higher taxes."

Why can you eliminate withstand? Withstand cannot be put in the sentence without changing the meaning of the sentence, so it is not a synonym for support.

Why can you eliminate suppose? Suppose sounds similar to support, but it does not mean the same thing and does not make sense in the sentence. Suppose is not a synonym for support.

Why can you eliminate consider? Consider cannot be put in the sentence without changing the meaning of the sentence, so it is not a synonym for support.

Which of the choices can be used in the sentence without changing the meaning? The correct answer is approve. Approve is a synonym for support.

Reading Vocabulary

Remember

If you have trouble answering a question, try these tips:

• Read all the choices first.

• Cross out the choices you know are wrong.

• If you crossed out only one or two choices, go back to the sentence.

• Reread the sentence, looking for clues to the meaning of the underlined word.

Example

Which word is a synonym for underline{humane}?

Your choices are A, underline{sympathetic}; B, underline{anguished}; C, underline{flimsy}; D, underline{hardy}.

_____

Write a sentence that uses the word underline{humane}.

_____

Which choices can you eliminate? Which of the choices can be used in your sentence without changing the meaning of the sentence?

_____

_____

_____

_____

_____

_____

_____

_____

Understanding Multiple-Meaning Words

Many words in English have more than one meaning and can be used as more than one part of speech, such as a noun, an adjective, or a verb. These words are called *multiple-meaning words*. It is important to know the multiple meanings of words and the situation in which they are used.

Here are some strategies to find a word that has the same meaning as a word in a given sentence.

1. Read the given sentence. Determine the meaning of the underlined word.

2. Determine the part of speech for the word: Is it used as a noun, an adjective, a verb, or something else?

3. Read all of the answer choices before selecting an answer.

4. Eliminate the choices where the meaning or part of speech is not the same.

Determining Correct Choices Suppose you are asked to identify a sentence in which the underlined word has the same meaning as the underlined word in the following sentence: "How much capital does the bank have on hand?"

First, ask yourself, "What does the word capital mean?" Capital means "money for starting a business."

Next, ask yourself, "What part of speech is capital used as in this sentence?" Capital is used as a noun.

Read these sentences. Then answer the questions.

> Austin is the capital of Texas.
>
> My neighbors have enough capital to start a small store.
>
> When you print your name, please use capital letters.

What does capital mean in the first sentence? As what part of speech is capital used? Capital means "the city or town where the government is located." Capital is used as a noun.

What does capital mean in the second sentence? As what part of speech is capital used? Capital means "money raised to start a business." Capital is used as a noun.

HINT

Remember that in order to find a multiple-meaning word that has the same meaning as it does in an example sentence, you must first determine the meaning of the word and its part of speech.

Reading Vocabulary

What does <u>capital</u> mean in the third sentence? As what part of speech is <u>capital</u> used? <u>Capital</u> means "an uppercase letter." <u>Capital</u> is used as an adjective.

The correct answer is the second sentence, because <u>capital</u> has the same meaning and is the same part of speech as the example sentence.

An Extra Example Here's another example. Suppose you are asked to identify a sentence in which the underlined word has the same meaning as the underlined word in the following sentence: "Please <u>staple</u> the pages together before handing in your paper."

First, ask yourself, "What does <u>staple</u> mean?" <u>Staple</u> means "put together with a metal wire."

Read these sentences. Then answer the question.

> My mother bought only <u>staple</u> groceries this time and not any special treats.

> The doctor sewed my cut together with a <u>staple</u>, instead of a stitch.

> Rice is a <u>staple</u> in the diet of many people of the world.

> Don't forget that you must <u>staple</u> the separate pieces of the project together.

What does <u>staple</u> mean in the first sentence? As what part of speech is <u>staple</u> used? <u>Staple</u> means "important." <u>Staple</u> is used as an adjective.

What does <u>staple</u> mean in the second sentence? As what part of speech is <u>staple</u> used? <u>Staple</u> means "a medical device." <u>Staple</u> is used as a noun.

What does <u>staple</u> mean in the third sentence? As what part of speech is <u>staple</u> used? <u>Staple</u> means "the most widely used crop." <u>Staple</u> is used as a noun.

What does <u>staple</u> mean in the fourth sentence? As what part of speech is <u>staple</u> used? <u>Staple</u> means "to assemble with a metal wire." <u>Staple</u> is used as a verb.

The correct answer is the fourth sentence because <u>staple</u> has the same meaning and is the same part of speech as in the example sentence.

Remember

Use a thesaurus to find meanings for words with multiple meanings. Check the exact meaning of the words in a dictionary.

Example

Read the following sentence. What does the word cue mean? As what part of speech is cue used?

The conductor gave a cue to his orchestra.

_____

What does the word cue mean in each of these sentences? As what part of speech is it used?

A The entertainer read from cue cards.

B As if on cue, the entire class began to run around the track.

C I'll cue you in when it is time for your solo.

D In the practice for the school play, the director explained the cue for each actor's entrance.

_____
_____
_____
_____
_____
_____
_____
_____
_____
_____
_____
_____
_____
_____

Reading Vocabulary

Analyzing Context Clues

A sentence that contains an unfamiliar word often provides clues to its meaning. The other words that provide these hints are known as *context clues*. Context clues suggest the general meaning of an unfamiliar word. Sometimes they even define the word.

Here are some ways to determine the meaning of a word using context clues from a sentence.

1. Read the sentence carefully.

2. Use the other words in the sentence as clues for the meaning of the word you don't know.

3. Read the sentence by switching the unfamiliar word with the possible answers and see which one makes sense.

4. Eliminate the incorrect choices.

Determining Correct Choices Suppose you are unfamiliar with the meaning of the underlined word in this sentence: "My prediction is that our team will win the World Series." Your answer choices are A, invitation; B, contract; C, forecast; or D, appeal.

The words *will win* indicate that winning is coming in the future.

Read the sentence using each of the meanings. Which choices can you eliminate? Choice A, invitation, is a note asking someone to come somewhere. Invitation does not make sense with the context clues. Invitation has nothing to do with winning.

Choice B, contract, is an agreement between two or more people to do something. Contract does not make sense with the context clues. Contract has nothing to do with winning.

Choice D, appeal, is a serious request for money, help, and so forth. Appeal does not make sense with the context clues. Appeal has nothing to do with winning.

None of these words indicate something that will happen in the future. Therefore, the correct answer is choice C. Forecast fits the idea and is a synonym for prediction.

Remember

Remember that finding the meaning of an unfamiliar word in a sentence means looking at the words in the rest of the sentence. They may be context clues.

HINT

Parts of speech are important in recognizing the meaning of a word in context. For example, sometimes a word will have a noun and a verb meaning as appeal does here. Be sure you are thinking of the right meaning when you try to fit the choice into the sentence. To test for a noun, try putting the word the before the word appeal.

An Extra Example Here's another example. Suppose you are unfamiliar with the meaning of the underlined word in the sentence, "Our former senator has won acclaim for his powers as a public speaker." Your answer choices are A, ambition; B, praise; C, amusement; D, merchandise.

The words *won*, *powers*, and *public speaker* indicate that the senator got a favorable judgment.

Read the sentence using each of the answer choices.

Choice A, ambition, is a strong desire to get something, such as wealth, fame, or power. Ambition does not make sense with the context clues. It has nothing to do with *public speaker*.

Choice C, amusement, means entertainment. It does not make sense with the context clues. Amusement has nothing to do with *powers*.

Choice D, merchandise, means goods that are bought and sold. It does not make sense with the context clues. Merchandise has nothing to do with *winning*, *powers*, or *public speaker*.

None of these indicate a favorable judgment. Therefore, the correct answer is Choice B. Praise fits the idea of the sentence and is a synonym for acclaim.

Additional Tips If you have trouble figuring out the answer to the question, try these suggestions:

- Read all the choices first.

- Cross out any choices you know are wrong.

- If you crossed out only one choice or two choices, reread the sentence.

- Look for clues to the meaning of the underlined word in the sentence.

Reading Vocabulary

Example

Read this sentence and look for clues that will help determine the meaning of the word <u>opulent</u>.

In the middle of the desert, the weary travelers dismounted from their camels and looked at the <u>opulent</u> palace, where the surprisingly splendid decorations promised welcome food and drink. <u>Opulent</u> means —

A neon   C fragile

B rich   D eternal

Which words in the sentence give you clues to the meaning of <u>opulent</u>?

_____

_____

Which answer choices do not make sense with the clue words? Which answer choice makes sense in the context of the sentence?

_____

_____

_____

_____

_____

_____

_____

_____

_____

_____

_____

Reading Vocabulary

DIRECTIONS ▶

Choose the word or group of words that means the same, or about the same, as the underlined word. Then mark the space for the answer you have chosen.

1

To <u>jiggle</u> is to —

A handle

B move

C shake

D climb

2

A <u>breed</u> is —

A a plank

B a wind

C a range

D a type

3

<u>Fame</u> means —

A reputation

B honor

C familiarity

D humor

4

To <u>lunge</u> is to —

A permit

B afford

C creep

D leap

Reading Vocabulary

DIRECTIONS ▶

Read the sentence in the box. Then choose the answer in which the underlined word is used in the same way. Mark the space for the answer you have chosen.

1

> The teacher's lecture covered the principle of supply and demand.

In which sentence does the word principle mean the same as the sentence above?

A Mr. Howard's neighbors regarded him as a man of principle.

B My decision to enter the contest is completely based on principle.

C What principle lead you to make that decision?

D Our system is based on the principle that all people are equal.

2

> Jan got an advance on her allowance.

In which sentence does the word advance mean the same as the sentence above?

A Advance the hands on the clock.

B The worker received an advance in order to pay his bills.

C She will advance to the rank of colonel within a year.

D The troops made an advance toward the city.

3

> The artist made a sketch of the picture before starting the painting.

In which sentence does the word sketch mean the same as the sentence above?

A Learning to sketch is not easy.

B The author's sketch describes an interesting setting.

C He will provide a sketch of the new restaurant for his client.

D Before you sketch the scene, examine it carefully.

4

> The members of the community made a pledge to give money to the theater.

In which sentence does the word pledge mean the same as the sentence above?

A You must sign a pledge that you will pay what you owe.

B We will recite the club's pledge.

C Everyone in the club should welcome the new pledge.

D The borrower must pledge a valuable possession for the loan.

DIRECTIONS ▶

As you read each sentence, use the other words in the sentence to help you figure out what the underlined word means. Then mark the space for the answer you have chosen.

1

Because my pants were too big, I asked my aunt to <u>alter</u> them. Alter means —

A tailor

B increase

C improve

D preserve

2

The desert plants died because they were unable to <u>adapt</u> to the changes in the weather. Adapt means —

A compare

B accept

C blunder

D adjust

3

<u>Concern</u> about storm clouds caused us to delay the picnic. Concern means —

A worry

B interest

C knowledge

D trouble

4

Lisa's best <u>quality</u> is that she is a trustworthy friend. Quality means —

A ability

B amount

C feature

D decision

Literary Reading Comprehension

Determining Causes and Effects

All good stories are made up of *events*. In other words, things happen. These happenings usually create the conflict, the rising action, and the climax in a story. They make the story interesting.

Explicit means stated directly. An *explicit cause* of an event is the reason that another event happens. An *explicit effect* of an event is something that happens as a result of another event happening first. To determine *explicit causes and effects*, you will first need to identify what happens in the story, and then determine what happened because those events ocurred. Once you do this, you will see the relationship between events in the story. Recognizing explicit causes and effects will make you a better reader.

> **HINT**
>
> Sometimes you can put the events in a story on a timeline to discover the explicit cause of the main event of a story.

Example

Read this passage.

Poor Jasper

   Like most cats, Jasper is curious. His curiosity always seems to get him in trouble. The other day I was filling up the bathtub, and my cat Jasper jumped up on the edge to see what was happening. The edge was slick, however, and he slid right into the tub. His legs and belly were soaked before he could hop back out. Poor Jasper!

Follow these steps to help you answer the question at the end of the lesson.

Step 1. Identify things that happen in the passage. This might involve identifying things that the author explains to have happened in the past, or it might involve identifying things that are happening as the story takes place. In this passage, Jasper the cat walks along the edge of the bathtub and slips into the water. Walking on the edge of the bathtub and slipping into the water are two events that happen in the passage.

Step 2. Identify the order in which the events in the passage occurred. In this passage, the author explains that Jasper first walked along the edge of the tub, and then he fell into the water. The author also explains that after he fell into the water, his legs and belly got soaked. Then he hopped out.

Step 3. Identify the reason why the events that happened did. In this passage, the author explains that the edge of the tub was slick. This indicates that the cause of Jasper falling into the water was his walking along a slick tub. To determine additional causes, simply follow the events in order.

Step 4. Now that you have determined the causes for events in the passage, switch things around to determine the effects. The effect of Jasper walking along the edge of a slick tub was that he fell into the water. To determine additional effects, follow the events in order.

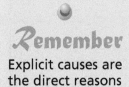

Remember

Explicit causes are the direct reasons that other events happen.

What is the cause of Jasper hopping out of the tub?

_____

_____

_____

What was the effect of Jasper getting soaking wet?

_____

_____

_____

Interpreting Figurative Language

Figurative language is intentionally different from the way we usually use words. Figurative language uses colorful words to create strong word pictures. Authors use figurative language in order to strengthen and freshen their message, to create a special effect, or to explore similarities between two things that are not generally alike.

There are many ways to use figurative language. Each way is usually colorful, surprising, and creative. When figurative language is used well, the author's ideas are hard to forget. Knowing how to interpret figurative language will make you a stronger reader.

Remember

Figurative language includes *similes*, comparisons of two unlike things using *like* or *as*. Figurative language also includes *metaphors*, which are similar to similes but do not use *like* or *as*.

Example

Read this passage.

Swim Like a Dolphin

His parents and his friends were cheering loudly from the stands. Trevor dove into the water and swam, a dolphin heading out to sea. He had prepared for this meet for a long time, and now he knew he could win the race.

Read this information to help you answer the question at the end of the lesson.

To understand how an author uses figurative language, follow these steps.

Step 1. Ask yourself who or what the passage about. Locating the main idea or the main character will help you understand what the descriptions mean. In this story, the passage is about a boy named Trevor swimming in a race.

Step 2. Look through the passage for any unusual or colorful language that stands out. This might mean looking for words that describe one thing that are usually used to describe something else, or it might mean looking for words that are not used in their true context. In this passage, look at the title, "Swim Like a Dolphin." Then notice how the author refers to Trevor as "a dolphin heading out to sea." This language is unusual because Trevor is not a dolphin. He is swimming, but he is not heading out to sea.

Step 3. Identify why the author uses the language that stands out. In this case, it is to compare two things; a boy swimming in a race and a dolphin swimming in the sea. A comparison between two unlike things is called a simile. Usually, authors use the words "like" or "as" to create similes. A boy is nothing like a dolphin, but in this case they both swim, and they share similar qualities. By saying Trevor *is* a dolphin, the author creates a metaphor. Trevor is not really a dolphin, but like a dolphin, he swims gracefully and quickly.

Remember

Figurative language helps describe the people and things in a story with colorful, descriptive words and comparisons.

How does the author use figurative language in this passage?

_____

_____

_____

_____

_____

Determining Details, Actions, or Sequence of Events

Good details make good stories. A description of how something looks or feels can bring a story to life for the reader. Some details are explicit—that is, they are spelled out for the reader. Other details, while not spelled out, are still important to the story and can be detected by a good reader. These are called *implicit details*.

A good author tries to tell a story in as few words as possible, making the remaining words more effective. Using implicit information helps an author accomplish this goal. By learning to recognize and interpret implicit information, a reader is better able to understand and enjoy the story.

HINT

A graphic organizer, such as a story map, can help you keep the details of the story in order.

Example

Read this passage.

Jasper Moves In

Jasper's curiosity often leads him to explore unusual places. We never know where we'll find Jasper. One day I found him on the top shelf of the cupboard. Apparently, my mother had accidentally left the door open. Luckily, he hadn't knocked down anything breakable. When I got out the step stool to rescue Jasper, he was purring. He is quite a jumper!

SKILL FOCUS

Read this information to help you answer the question at the end of the lesson.

To discover the implied sequence of events, follow these steps.

Step 1. Identify the main idea of the passage. This passage is about a cat named Jasper, who is sitting on the top shelf of a cupboard.

Step 2. Identify the events in the passage. The events will involve specific actions and details. In this story, the events are:

The author finds Jasper on the top shelf of the cupboard.
The author's mother had accidentally left the cupboard door open.
Jasper hadn't knocked down anything breakable.
Jasper was purring when the author helped the cat down.

Step 3. Put the events of the passage in chronological order. This means putting them in the order in which they occurred. Keep in mind that authors do not always relate the events in a story in the order they occurred. Sometimes, they relate the events out of order, but you can easily recognize the order if you understand what the author is trying to say. In this passage, you understand that the events took place in this order:

The mother leaves the cupboard door open.
The author finds the cat.
The author gets a step stool to get the cat down.
The cat purrs.

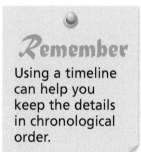

Remember

Using a timeline can help you keep the details in chronological order.

Step 4. Determine what the author suggests but does not say. Ask yourself what must have happened if the events in the story happened as the author said they did. In this passage, Jasper was already in the cupboard when the story began. Ask yourself what must have happened if Jasper was in the cupboard. He had to get up there somehow. The author tells you that the mother left the cupboard door open. The author also tells you that Jasper is a good jumper. In this way, the author suggests or implies what happened before Jasper got in the cupboard.

What action is implied in the passage's sequence of events?

_____

_____

Discerning Author's Voice

An author's *voice* is the way the author talks about a subject. That voice reveals the author's personality, beliefs, or feelings about a subject. For example, an author who writes stories sometimes uses the story's characters to get a particular message across. The way an author describes the characters and tells about their thoughts and feelings shows the concerns the author has about a subject.

To *discern* an author's voice means to find out about the author's personality, beliefs, or feelings through the literature he or she has written. Think of this example: If an author writes a sad story about very poor characters, the author may want readers to imagine what it feels like to be so poor. The author's voice, speaking through the characters, may encourage readers to care about the subject as deeply as the author does.

Remember

Usually an author does not speak directly to readers in stories. You have to interpret the author's voice from the way the story is written.

Example

Read this passage.

Jessica's Move

Last summer, Jessica's family moved to a different town. All summer long, Jessica was anxious about going to her new school. She knew it would feel like starting over in the lowest grade. She would have to learn how to find her locker and her classes all over again. She would have to make new friends after losing friends she had known for many years. What if the new kids didn't like her?

Read this information to help you answer the question at the end of the lesson.

To find out about the author's voice, use the following steps.

Step 1. Decide what is the main idea of the passage. In this passage, Jessica has moved to a new town and she worries all summer about starting at a new school.

Step 2. Look for details in the passage that support the main idea. In the passage "Jessica's Move," the details that show Jessica's thoughts and feelings are:

She feels like going to the new school would be like starting all over in the lowest grade. She will have to learn where her locker and classes are. She will have to make new friends.

Step 3. Draw a conclusion about Jessica's thoughts and feelings. Are those thoughts and feelings ones that you recognize as real? For this passage, you might conclude that Jessica's worry and loneliness are real because you have had similar thoughts and feelings.

Step 4. Ask yourself a question about the author's thoughts and feelings based on the way the character is described. For example, thinking about this passage, ask yourself how the author feels about Jessica. From the description of Jessica, you might reasonably decide that the author cares about Jessica and is sympathetic to her situation.

HINT

Look for words and phrases that show how an author feels about the characters. The question *What if the new kids didn't like her?* shows Jessica's worries and the author's sympathy for her.

What evidence points to the author's voice in this passage?

_____

_____

_____

_____

_____

_____

A Friend for Alice

When Alice turned six, her parents gave her a box with holes in it for a birthday present. "You should open this one right away," said her dad, smiling.

Alice untied the ribbon and lifted the lid—and out leaped a tan puppy with brown ears, a black nose, and a long tail. Alice exclaimed happily, "You remembered! But I didn't think you'd get me a dog."

"Your father and I talked about it," said Alice's mom. "You have to promise to take care of this little girl, to feed her and walk her—even when you don't want to—and to teach her how to mind her manners."

"I promise," said Alice, who couldn't take her eyes from the puppy's smiling face. As the puppy licked Alice's hand, Alice thought long and hard. "Your fur is light brown, like sand on the beach," she told the puppy. "I think I will call you Sandra." The name stuck.

As Alice and Sandra grew up together, Sandra proved that a dog really can be a best friend. Once, on a hike in the woods behind her house, Alice got her foot wedged between two rocks and couldn't get loose. Once Sandra realized it wasn't a game, she raced home to get Alice's dad, who came running as soon as he understood the situation. Another time, she barked loudly at a suspicious person near the house.

"Good girl, Sandra," said Alice. "You're the best dog in the whole world."

Of course, Sandra was not good all the time. As she became a full-grown dog, Alice had to teach her not to take food from the table. Also, Sandra had to learn not to jump joyfully on the people who came to visit Alice's home. Eventually Sandra learned she could get away with leaning quietly against the seated visitor's legs and waiting for an ear rub.

Alice remembered her promise and always walked and fed Sandra first thing, even on days when she wanted to sleep late or do something else.

On her fourteenth birthday, Alice received a tennis racket and a great pair of jeans. "Thanks, Mom and Dad," she said happily.

At her feet lay Sandra, who was having one of her frequent naps. Sandra didn't zip through the woods during their walks anymore, instead letting Alice set the pace. Sometimes she didn't even chase the squirrels darting across her path. She ate her food at a leisurely pace, and she wasn't quite as slim as she used to be. Sometimes, though, she still got a little too excited when visitors came over.

"Some things never change," said Alice, smiling.

1

Why does Sandra run to get Alice's father?

A A squirrel has darted across the path.

B A visitor is knocking on the door.

C Alice has wedged her foot between two rocks.

D Alice is neglecting her responsibilities.

2

Why does Alice say Sandra is the best dog in the world?

A Alice is proud of Sandra.

B Alice's parents are proud of Sandra.

C Sandra has won an international contest.

D Sandra's breed is noted for intelligence.

3

What do Sandra's naps, slower pace, and weight gain suggest?

A She has a mild illness.

B She is concerned about Alice.

C She is expecting a litter of puppies.

D She is getting older.

4

What does the author think about dogs?

A Dogs and cats make equally good pets.

B Dogs are dangerous to the local wildlife.

C Dogs are useful work animals.

D Dogs truly are humans' best friend.

Informational Reading Comprehension

Drawing Conclusions

When reading a passage, the reader sometimes must figure out what the passage means by *drawing conclusions* from details in the passage. If an idea in the passage is not clearly stated, the reader has to use what *is* clearly stated to figure out what is not.

For example, imagine seeing a woman working in a yard. You ask her how she is doing. She says, "Okay," but you notice sweat dripping from her face and dark circles under her eyes. From these details, you could draw the conclusion that she is okay but also very tired.

Remember

Drawing conclusions from details requires "reading between the lines." Do you get the feeling there are more ideas in a passage than just what is written? Ask yourself these questions:

• What feeling do I get from reading this passage?

• What details in the passage support that feeling?

Example

Read this passage.

Everyone Speaks the Language

Have you ever heard your teachers say that they need to have a "tête-á-tête" with your parents? Have you ever had a "rendezvous" with anyone near the "Rio Grande" in Texas?

If you have, you have used or heard words in English that are borrowed from languages in other countries. The words *rendezvous* and *tête-á-tête* come from French, while *Rio Grande* and even *Texas* come from Spanish. At some point in history, France, Spain, and Mexico all had colonies in what is now the United States.

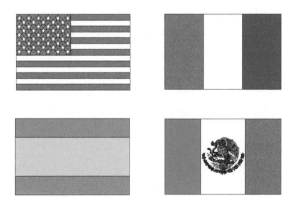

Read this information to help you answer the question at the end of the lesson.

To draw a conclusion about the presence of French and Spanish words in the English language, follow these steps.

Step 1: Study the details in the passage to gain an understanding of what the author clearly explains. In this passage, perhaps you recognize the words *Rio Grande* and *rendezvous*. The author clearly explains that these are words that come from the Spanish and French languages that have now become familiar words among English speakers. English speakers often use these foreign words in English phrases. In the passage, the author uses the words *Rio Grande* and *rendezvous* as details that explain important ideas. The author explains that these words are borrowed from other languages, but also the author explains that France, Spain and Mexico had colonies in what is now the United States.

Step 2: Identify other ideas in the passage that the author does not clearly explain. For example, the author does not explain that people who settled in the United States came mainly from England, nor does the author explain that they brought their native language with them. The author does not explain that English became the language spoken by most of the people in what became the United States, either, but you probably know that all of these things are true.

Step 3: Use details from the passage to draw conclusions. For instance, you might conclude that English speakers in the United States borrowed words from the French, Spanish, and Mexican colonists. You might also conclude that many other words commonly used in English phrases were also borrowed from other languages.

> ## HINT
> Not every detail in a passage will be helpful in drawing conclusions.

Why are French and Spanish words used in the English language?

_____

_____

_____

_____

_____

Providing Support for Conclusions

When you provide support for a conclusion, you look in a passage for details that show that your conclusion is true. For example, look at the following sentence: The soft hum of the engine had soothed Sheila to sleep, but when she awoke to see mountains passing beneath the wing outside her window, she remembered why she had been nervous in the first place.

Even though the word is never actually written in the sentence, you can tell that Sheila is in an airplane. How can you tell? You *draw a conclusion* based on details. Take note of the particular details on which you based your conclusion. For example, the following details *provide support* for the conclusion that Sheila is flying in an airplane: The engine hums. There are mountains *beneath* her. There is a wing outside her window. Sheila is nervous.

Remember

Details in a passage can also be used to provide support for a conclusion about what you think may happen in the future, beyond what is written in the passage.

Example

Read this passage.

Money Talks

Thousands of years ago, human beings traded items to get what they wanted. When people began to find uses for metals, they created coins to use for trading. These coins were symbols of the goods humans used to trade for other goods. Carrying around heavy coins became difficult, and humans invented money made of paper. They then traded the paper money for items they needed. Soon, they found they could write a  note promising to pay for the items at a later time. These "checks" were even easier than carrying around paper money. Then came a piece of plastic. The plastic card is like a check except that people do not have to take the time to write anything except their name. That is the easiest way so far to exchange goods.

Read this information to help you answer the question at the end of the lesson.

Step 1: Look for the details of the passage. The details from the passage show that at first people traded goods for goods. Then they turned metal into coins. Next they used paper money, followed by checks, and finally plastic credit cards. Coins replaced goods. Paper replaced coins. Plastic may replace paper.

Step 2: Using the details from the passage and what you already know about a subject, draw a conclusion based on the details of the passage. For example, you could draw a conclusion about the different kinds of money that people have chosen to use in history. The details in the passage and what you already know about the subject lead to a conclusion that people choose the kind of money to use based on what is available and what they like.

Step 3: Ask yourself what details in the passage support your conclusion. Drawing a conclusion based on details shows that people like to use the most convenient way to exchange their money for goods. For the most part, that desire for convenience has led people to invent several types of money that are easier to carry and use. The passage lists several types of money—goods, metal coins, paper bills and checks, and plastic cards. The several types of money are the details that support your conclusion.

Remember

Using details to support a conclusion is a back-and-forth process. Use details to draw a conclusion. Then note the details that led you to that conclusion. Use the details to provide the support for that conclusion.

> What details from the paragraph support the conclusion that humans will one day stop using actual money altogether or invent a new kind of money?
>
> _____
>
> _____
>
> _____
>
> _____
>
> _____
>
> _____
>
> _____

Analyzing Text Structure

The *text structure* of a passage refers to the way the author puts together the passage. Some informational passages have an introduction followed by different sections, or paragraphs, to support that introduction. The introduction may take several forms, such as a quotation placed below the title. Some fiction passages use a character's dialogue to move the plot of the story forward.

When you read a passage, *analyze* the structure of the passage to help you understand the ideas the author wants to express. Ask yourself if the structure makes those ideas clearer.

Remember

As you read passages on tests, think about the structure of your own writing. Does the passage have an introduction and supporting paragraphs? Does each of the paragraphs have a topic sentence? Can you use the same structure in your own writing?

Example

Read this passage.

Man of Action

"True individual freedom cannot exist without economic security and independence. People who are hungry and out of a job are the stuff of which dictatorships are made."
—Franklin Delano Roosevelt, 32nd President of the United States

Within that quotation from a speech Roosevelt made to Congress lie the main issues of Roosevelt's time in office. He was first elected president in 1932, in the heart of the Great Depression. Many people were hungry or unemployed, so Roosevelt tried to solve these problems. In 1941, one year after being elected president for the third time, Roosevelt faced his greatest challenge: war against the dictatorships of imperial Japan and Nazi Germany. He met the challenge as he met every other one—with ideas and leadership.

Read this information to help you answer the question at the end of the lesson.

Step 1: To analyze the text structure, ask yourself what the different parts of the text are. In this passage, the author has used a title, a quotation by Roosevelt, and a paragraph. You can recognize the title and the quotation because they look different from the paragraph.

Step 2: Determine the main idea of each different part. For example, in the quotation Roosevelt is saying that terrible economic problems can lead to even more serious political problems within a country. It grabs attention and tells the reader what the passage will be about.

In the paragraph, the author says that Roosevelt had to face the economic problems of the Great Depression and war against the dictatorships of imperial Japan and Nazi Germany. Roosevelt tried to solve the economic problems with his good ideas and leadership. Those same qualities carried over into his battle against dictatorships.

Step 3: Think about the relationship between the different parts of the text. Notice that the main idea of the quotation shows that Roosevelt knew he had serious problems he wanted to solve. The main idea of the paragraph shows that Roosevelt used his knowledge and his abilities to solve the economic problems in 1932, and to face other political difficulties in 1941. These two different parts of the text talk about the same thing—the problems that Roosevelt had and the way he tried to solve them.

Remember

An analysis of the text structure:

1. breaks the text apart to find out how the parts are related

2. finds the main idea of each part

3. explains how the parts are related

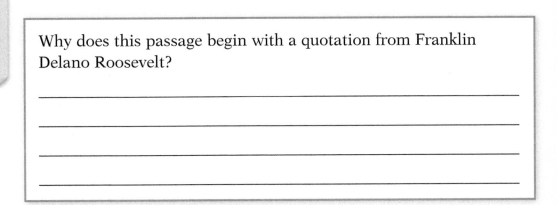

Why does this passage begin with a quotation from Franklin Delano Roosevelt?

_____

_____

_____

_____

Asking Clarifying Questions

Learning to ask the right questions will help you understand the passage you are reading. *Clarifying questions* are questions the reader asks to gain a better understanding of the passage. Sometimes, authors anticipate readers' questions and answer them in the course of their writing. Other times, authors leave questions unanswered, however. In these cases, asking clarifying questions helps you get the information you need to make sense of what you're reading.

Sometimes a passage introduces a topic you have never heard of before. You might have questions about the topic as you read. This does not mean the author did not do a good job of writing the material. Sometimes, it means that the author has succeeded in stimulating your interest. Asking clarifying questions often involves doing a little research on your own that might lead you to additional information you might find of interest as well.

HINT

Do you have any experience with the subject of the passage you are reading? Are any sections of the passage confusing? If you answered *yes*, then what can you ask to help you better understand the passage?

Example

Read this passage.

The Alligator and Its Relatives

Like its relatives the crocodile and the caiman, the alligator is part of the reptile family. These reptiles are meat eaters, and they have short, strong legs and powerful tails. They also have long snouts with rows of sharp teeth, including extra-long teeth in the bottom rows. The largest of these reptiles grow between 12 and 18 feet long.

The caiman and the crocodile can be found as far south as Central and South America, but the alligator lives primarily in the southeastern United States. Alligators and their relatives are often unafraid of humans, so if you see one loose in the wild, you should stay far away from it.

Read this information to help you answer the question at the end of the lesson.

To ask a clarifying question, follow these steps.

Step 1: Read the passage and determine the main idea. The passage is about alligators.

Step 2: Notice the details of the passage. In this passage you learn that alligators are members of the reptile family. They are kin to crocodiles and caimans, but they live in the southwestern United States. You also learn that they are meat eaters, that they are large and strong, that they have lots of teeth, and that they are often unafraid of humans.

Step 3: Decide if there are any details in the passage that are unclear or confusing. Did the author leave questions unanswered or stimulate ideas that led you to want to know more? The author of this passage explains that the alligator has strong legs, a powerful tail, and many sharp teeth. The alligator can grow larger than a human. It is not afraid of humans.

Step 4: Ask a clarifying question about those details. For example, you may want to know if alligators are dangerous to humans and, if so, where alligators live. You might also want to know how alligators compare with crocodiles and caimans. Do crocodiles and caimans look similar to alligators, and are they dangerous to humans as well?

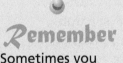

Remember

Sometimes you may have to answer your clarifying question by going to a source outside the text and doing research. For example, to find out where the alligator lives you may need to do research in the library.

What clarifying question could you ask to find out more information about the alligator and its relatives?

_____

_____

_____

_____

_____

_____

It's a Small Continent

Imagine taking a train from Amarillo, Texas, to Dallas, Texas. How many different countries would you pass through on the six-hour trip? One, of course, because you would be in the United States for the entire trip. In fact, you would stay in the state of Texas for the course of the trip. What if you decided, however, to take a train trip from Bastogne (ba-ston´), Belgium, to Trier, Germany, and then up the Marne River to Paris, France? During this trip, you would pass through mountains, valleys, and four separate countries. Yet, it would take you about the same amount of time as a trip from Amarillo to Dallas. This example shows how closely tied almost every country in Europe is, geographically speaking, and how different the feeling of traveling in Europe is from traveling here in the United States.

Your trip begins in Bastogne, Belgium, a town situated in southeastern Belgium, very near the border with Luxembourg. During World War II, Allied forces defeated the Germans at the Battle of the Bulge not far from Bastogne. Very few wars were fought in either Amarillo, Texas, or Dallas, Texas. The train to Trier, Germany, makes its way into the Ardennes (är-den') Mountains, where if you are lucky you might see a wild boar chasing a lynx.

You just manage to close your eyes for what seems like a moment, when someone nudges you awake and points out the window. As you look, all you can see are trees just like the ones you were looking at when you closed your eyes. However, before you can ask what you are supposed to be looking at, someone tells you that was Luxembourg. When you closed your eyes for half an hour, you missed an entire country!

The train pulls into the station in Trier, Germany, and you get out to look around. Trier is the oldest city in the country, founded around the year A.D. 15 by the Romans. Many of the buildings, especially the churches, are still standing from Roman times, almost 2,000 years ago. The oldest building in Texas is less than 300 years old—quite a difference.

The trip from Trier to Paris takes quite a bit longer, although you cross from Germany into France within about an hour. With the Marne River, the largest branch of the Seine, on the left side of the train, you enjoy the trip through rolling hills and beautiful farms. As you pull into the station in Paris, you check your watch. The entire trip has taken a little less than six hours, and you try to remember your last trip from Amarillo to Dallas. Then it comes back to you: You slept through it.

1

The structure of the passage makes the reader feel —

A as though Texas is smaller than it looks

B as though the train is a slow way to travel

C as though he or she is learning about Europe

D as though he or she is taking a trip through Europe

2

Which shows that Luxembourg is between Belgium and Germany?

A The train begins in Belgium and ends in France.

B The train moves through Luxembourg so quickly.

C The train goes through Luxembourg on the way to Germany.

D The train moves from southern Belgium to northern Germany.

3

To learn more details about the time spent in Luxembourg, the reader should ask —

A the length of the Marne River

B how wide the country is in miles

C how far the country is from Belgium

D the length of the Ardennes Mountains

4

According to the passage, Germany was —

A once Roman

B once French

C filled with wild boars

D filled with old churches

Functional Reading Comprehension

Forming a Hypothesis

A *hypothesis* is a guess or theory that can be checked through more investigation. Scientists form hypotheses about how the world works. Then they develop scientific experiments to determine if their hypotheses are correct.

You can form a hypothesis about an idea from something you read, because the idea raises an interesting question. You might investigate your hypothesis by reading more, talking with a friend, or checking other references. Later you would decide if you have enough information to decide if your hypothesis is correct.

> **HINT**
>
> You can begin to form a hypothesis by:
>
> 1. noting interesting ideas in the passage
>
> 2. jotting down any questions that these ideas raise

Example

Read this passage.

Recent Sightings of Mountain Lions

Members of the cat family, mountain lions are among the biggest wild animals that roam the American wilderness. Also known as cougars, panthers, and pumas, mountain lions hunt deer and elk, as well as smaller, older, or sick animals. These big cats have also been known to kill sheep and cattle. For this

reason, mountain lions have been driven away from ranches and livestock herds. During the last century, mountain lion populations dropped dramatically. Some scientists feared the big cats would disappear forever. Recently,

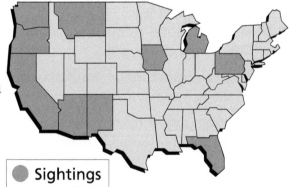

● Sightings

however, mountain lions have appeared in some surprising places, from the outskirts of Los Angeles to a cornfield in Iowa. They are found in the wild in places as distant from each other as Washington state and Florida. These cats are shy animals and prefer to hunt at night when they can surprise their prey, so your chances of spotting one are still pretty slim.

Read this information to help you answer the question at the end of the lesson.

Use the following steps to help you form a hypothesis.

Step 1: Identify the main idea of the passage. This passage is about mountain lions. It includes a map and information about what animals the mountain lions hunt and where the mountain lions live.

Step 2: Identify any interesting ideas within the passage. The interesting ideas in this passage include information about the disappearance of mountain lions. The author explains that the mountain lion population dropped so dramatically that people thought the mountain lions were disappearing. The author uses a map to explain that the animals seem to be back and showing up in some surprising places.

Step 3: Identify any questions that these ideas raise. For example, you could ask: Are the mountain lions *really* back? Why? If they're so shy, why are they showing up in populated areas? Do they need food or are they becoming more comfortable around people? Different people might have different questions, depending on what ideas they find most interesting.

Step 4: To form a hypothesis, make a guess based on the ideas in the passage and the questions that the ideas raise. Your hypothesis may be a statement that can later be proved by further research.

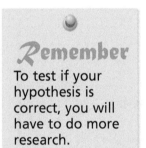

Remember
To test if your hypothesis is correct, you will have to do more research.

What hypothesis might you form from this passage?

_____

_____

_____

_____

_____

_____

Identifying Characteristics of Genre

A literary *genre* is a type of literature. The four main literary genres are fiction, nonfiction, poetry, and drama. Identifying the characteristics of a genre means understanding what is special about that genre.

For example, the nonfiction genre deals with real events, places, people, and things. This information is usually developed using facts, or statements that can be proved or supported. Examples of nonfiction include biographies, essays, newspaper and magazine articles, letters, advertising, and research reports.

> ### HINT
>
> To distinguish nonfiction from fiction, ask if what you are reading 1) deals with real events, places, people, and things and 2) relays the information in a factual way.

Example

Read this passage.

Weather Conditions in Massachusetts

	Boston	Adams
Average July Temperature	73.4°	67.2°
Average January Temperature	28.6°	18.4°
Average Precipitation (inches per year)	38.2	49.1

Many people are surprised to learn that, in the winter, western Massachusetts is usually colder than the eastern portion of the state. People are surprised because they assume that the Atlantic Ocean, along the state's eastern edge, has a cooling effect. The state's western hills, however, are colder. The lowest temperature ever recorded in the state is −34°F (−36.6° C). This occurred on the western side at Birch Hill Dam on January 18, 1957. Average January temperatures range from above 30°F (−1° C) in the east to below 22°F (−6° C) in the west. The highest temperature, 107°F (41.6° C), was recorded at Chester and New Bedford on August 2, 1975. During the summer, temperatures in the center of the state range from an average high of 72°F (22° C) or above to below 70°F (21° C).

Read this information to help you answer the question at the end of the lesson.

Follow these steps to identify the genre of a passage.

Step 1: Take note of the characteristics of a passage. Ask yourself if the passage deals with real events, places, people, and things. In this passage this table and the following information is about a real place (Massachusetts) and real events (average high and low temperatures).

Step 2: Decide where the passage might appear. The information in this passage might appear in a report on Massachusetts's weather or in a magazine or encyclopedia article on Massachusetts. Reports and encyclopedias contain nonfiction information.

Step 3: Examine any supporting information that might help determine the genre. For example, the illustration, or table, adds important details to the presentation of information. By showing the average temperature and rainfall of the state in January and July, the illustration supports the article's facts about Massachusetts's weather. The text and illustration present information about the state's climate in a factual way by listing average temperatures and precipitation.

Step 4: Think about the language that the passage uses. Usually nonfiction uses straightforward, unemotional words.

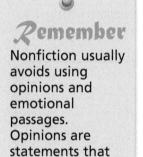

Remember

Nonfiction usually avoids using opinions and emotional passages. Opinions are statements that cannot be proved.

Based on its characteristics, what is the genre of this passage?

_____

_____

_____

_____

_____

_____

_____

Choosing Appropriate Reading Strategies

Reading strategies are various ways to read any kind of writing, from books and plays, to newspapers, advertising, and labels. Good readers choose reading strategies that are right for their purpose and the text they are reading.

Examples of reading strategies include *scanning*, *skimming*, and *reading carefully*. Most people *read carefully* because they are interested or because they are reading for information. These careful readers focus on the title, headings, words in special type, the first sentence of each paragraph, and any illustrations. While reading, these people may take notes to refer to later. *Scanning* is used for searching text quickly for a piece of information, such as a definition or special word. *Skimming* is used for reading parts of the text in order to get a sense of the content.

As you read the text that follows, imagine that you are researching the geography of Mexico for a report.

> ## HINT
>
> Know your reading purpose. The reading strategy you choose depends on your purpose for reading.

Examples

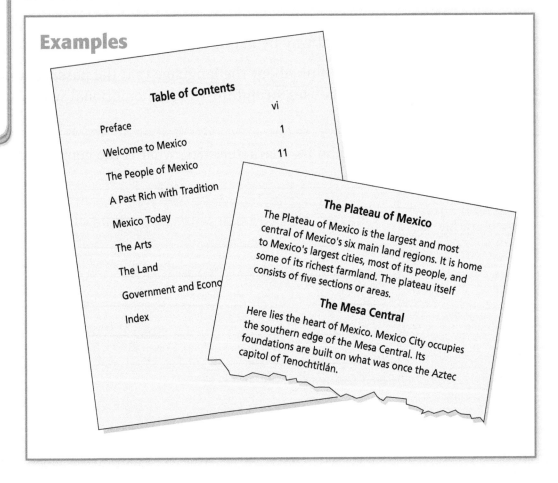

Table of Contents

The Plateau of Mexico

The Plateau of Mexico is the largest and most central of Mexico's six main land regions. It is home to Mexico's largest cities, most of its people, and some of its richest farmland. The plateau itself consists of five sections or areas.

The Mesa Central

Here lies the heart of Mexico. Mexico City occupies the southern edge of the Mesa Central. Its foundations are built on what was once the Aztec capitol of Tenochtitlán.

SKILL FOCUS

Read this information to help you answer the question at the end of the lesson.

To decide on a reading strategy, or strategies, follow these steps.

Step 1: Decide upon your purpose for reading. In this example, you may be reading for information about the geography of Mexico.

Step 2: Examine the different parts of the passage. For example, the book's table of contents looks different from the information in a chapter from the book. To find information about the land in Mexico, scan the Table of Contents.

The chapter in the book uses headings and subheadings to organize its information. Think of your social studies textbook. Usually information in a social studies text is organized so that a student can find information easily. The subheadings "The Plateau of Mexico" and "The Mesa Central" help a student locate specific information easily and quickly. After you find sections of information, you may read more slowly, taking notes on what you are reading.

Step 3: Decide which reading strategy might be the best for each part of the passage. To look for key words, such as *geography* and *land*, you would use a different reading strategy from the one in which you read for information necessary for a social studies test. To preview the chapter, you could skim headings, key words, and illustrations for useful information. If you decide the article will be helpful, then read carefully and take notes.

*R*emember

Scanning is reading quickly for specific information.

Skimming is reading quickly to get an overview of what the passage is about.

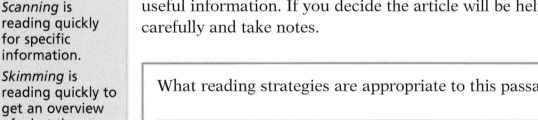

What reading strategies are appropriate to this passage?

_____

_____

_____

_____

_____

Isle Royale

Location

In the northwest corner of Lake Superior lies Isle Royale. Made up of a main island and dozens of smaller islands, Isle Royale is also a National Park. There is no bridge to Isle Royale, so park visitors must reach it by boat or floatplane.

Early Inhabitants

Inhabitants of the island include squirrels, hares, beaver, fox, timber wolves, and moose. The wolf and the moose, however, are relatively recent arrivals. About a hundred years ago, the first moose probably swam to Isle Royale from Canada searching for feeding grounds.

Population Cycles of Moose

At that time, none of the island's other animals hunted moose. This meant that the moose population could grow much faster than it normally would. By 1930 the moose numbered between 1,000 and 3,000. That's a lot of moose for a small island! As the moose population grew, their food source became scarce. Many moose starved or became ill and died. Wildfires killed more animals, and soon the moose population was about 450 animals. As the island recovered from the fire, however, so did the moose population. With fewer moose and more to eat, the moose population began to soar.

The Ice Bridge

These cycles might have continued, except for a new arrival during the winter of 1948 through 1949. That winter, an ice bridge formed between Canada and the island. A small pack of timber wolves crossed from the mainland.

Natural Enemies

Wolves hunt moose for food. So when the wolves reached the island, they decided to stay. Since then, the original wolf pack has produced more packs. The wolves help keep the moose population steady by removing the sick and the old. The moose provide just enough food for the wolves to keep their population in balance. So the presence of two natural enemies, the moose and the wolf, benefits both in many ways.

Complete Encyclopedia

1

A reader looking for information about fishing on Isle Royale might —

A read the passage carefully

B take notes on the passage for a report

C scan the passage for related information

D skim the passage for information on moose and wolves

2

The first sentence helps identify the passage as nonfiction because the sentence —

A is clear

B states a fact

C appeals to the senses

D introduces the setting

3

Based on this passage, a reader might form a hypothesis that —

A taking a floatplane to Isle Royale is dangerous

B the relationship between wolves and dogs is unique

C the moose arrived on Isle Royale a number of years ago

D other natural enemies benefit each other

4

A reader who was interested only in the size of Isle Royale *probably* would —

A skip the passage

B examine the map

C read the passage carefully

D skim the passage for an overview

Reading Vocabulary

DIRECTIONS ▶

Choose the word or group of words that means the same, or about the same, as the underlined word. Then mark the space for the answer you have chosen.

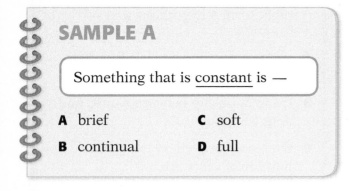

SAMPLE A

Something that is <u>constant</u> is —

A brief   **C** soft

B continual   **D** full

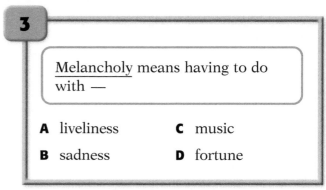

3

<u>Melancholy</u> means having to do with —

A liveliness   **C** music

B sadness   **D** fortune

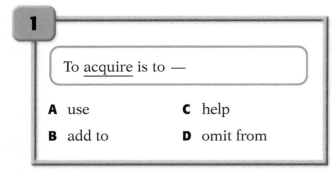

1

To <u>acquire</u> is to —

A use   **C** help

B add to   **D** omit from

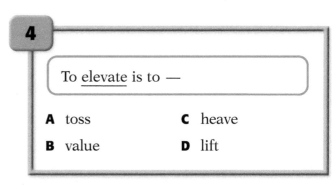

4

To <u>elevate</u> is to —

A toss   **C** heave

B value   **D** lift

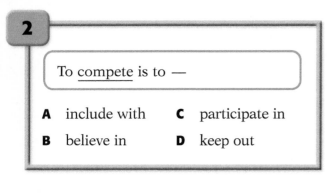

2

To <u>compete</u> is to —

A include with   **C** participate in

B believe in   **D** keep out

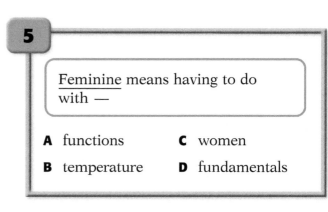

5

<u>Feminine</u> means having to do with —

A functions   **C** women

B temperature   **D** fundamentals

6

A hermit is most like a —

A loner   **C** helmet

B hostage   **D** director

7

Something that is infinite is —

A cruel   **C** unexpected

B vast   **D** insecure

8

To scour is to —

A choose   **C** answer

B frown   **D** clean

9

To imply something is to —

A suggest   **C** hustle

B rule   **D** include

10

A menace is a —

A nominee   **C** terminal

B threat   **D** novelty

11

Something that is favorable is —

A desirable   **C** avoidable

B sanitary   **D** negative

12

Something that is plentiful is —

A barren   **C** appropriate

B eternal   **D** abundant

DIRECTIONS ▷

Read the sentence in the box. Then choose the answer in which the underlined word is used in the same way. Mark the space for the answer you have chosen.

SAMPLE B

> Which candidate will you back for class president?

In which sentence does the word back mean the same as in the sentence above?

A The kitchen is at the back of the house.

B Back up slowly so you don't fall.

C My dad has a sore back.

D My family will back the American League team in the World Series.

13

> How many yards did the quarterback gain on that play?

In which sentence does the word gain mean the same as in the sentence above?

A We hope to gain three hundred points during the competition.

B Dad made a gain of five hundred dollars on the sale of the furniture.

C Our grandfather clock seems to gain five minutes a week.

D She stood to gain a fortune if the lawsuit was settled.

14

> My assignment came back from my teacher without a mark on it.

In which sentence does the word mark mean the same as in the sentence above?

A The coach hit the mark when she named Jane to the first squad.

B Mark my words; the winner of the event will be Marcus.

C Did you remember to mark your calendar for the big game?

D Mom will be upset if she sees a mark anywhere on the table.

15

> The parade will be over by the time it is dark outside.

In which sentence does the word by mean the same as in the sentence above?

A Mother said to be home by 5:00.

B My dad's office is by the stadium.

C Time flew by while we were decorating the gym.

D That short story was written by my favorite author.

16

Dad likes to jog for twenty minutes as part of his workout routine.

In which sentence does the word jog mean the same as in the sentence above?

A How can I jog your memory about the accident?

B It's a long jog to the park from the school.

C Don't jog his arm; he'll spill the juice.

D Do you jog to stay in shape?

17

Narrow your choices by eliminating wrong answers.

In which sentence does the word narrow mean the same as in the sentence above?

A The narrow passage through the woods was quite dark.

B The candidate won by a narrow majority.

C "Narrow the margin on this essay," the teacher said.

D Try not to have a narrow mind when you make your choice.

18

Please get a needle and sew a button on this shirt.

In which sentence does the word needle mean the same as in the sentence above?

A The sewing machine needle is too dull to sew leather.

B Does the needle of the compass always point north?

C Don't needle your brother; he's not bothering you.

D A pine needle fell from the fir tree in our neighbor's yard.

19

The lead in the play is Mark.

In which sentence does the word lead mean the same as in the sentence above?

A Lead the way; I can't see without my glasses.

B Did we choose Anna as the lead on the project?

C Lead with an ace if you want to win the card game.

D Joe likes to lead with his left when he boxes.

20

> Our favorite store will lower the prices of shoes this weekend.

In which sentence does the word lower mean the same as in the sentence above?

A Which rank is lower, captain or major?

B Hopefully, that company will lower demands on its employees.

C Which singer produces a lower sound, a tenor or a bass?

D Lower the window; it's cold in here.

21

> Tammy has a pleasant singing voice.

In which sentence does the word voice mean the same as in the sentence above?

A Mark's voice was hard to understand because of his illness.

B Don't complain if you didn't voice an opinion.

C The candidate claims to be the voice of the people.

D Daniel wants to take voice lessons.

DIRECTIONS ▶

As you read each sentence, use the other words in the sentence to help you figure out what the underlined word means. Then mark the space for the answer you have chosen.

SAMPLE C

Hal _astutely_ presented a clever solution to the problem. _Astutely_ means —

A shrewdly   **C** angrily

B openly   **D** casually

24

We were surprised by the _temerity_ of the speaker, who is usually very dull. _Temerity_ means —

A boldness   **C** vocabulary

B thoughtfulness   **D** appearance

22

I'm surprised such a creative person could make such a _banal_ remark. _Banal_ means —

A dull   **C** rude

B long   **D** helpful

25

The tasty-looking meal _tantalized_ the dieter. _Tantalized_ means —

A alerted   **C** tormented

B awakened   **D** targeted

23

The comedian's _banter_ kept us all laughing. _Banter_ means —

A clothing   **C** mood

B joking   **D** attitude

26

The _volume_ of the hoop skirt filled the carriage. _Volume_ means —

A fullness   **C** silkiness

B stiffness   **D** softness

27

Maria made the absurd statement that dogs can talk. Absurd means —

A wonderful   **C** foolish

B polite   **D** specific

28

The engineer created a prototype of the bridge he was planning. Prototype means —

A stamp   **C** model

B painting   **D** spectacle

29

Do you think a somnambulist knows what hazards to avoid or can the person actually see? Somnambulist means —

A security guard   **C** teacher

B sleepwalker   **D** truck driver

30

Can a person who walks on nails really transcend pain? Transcend means —

A arrange   **C** suffer

B avoid   **D** surpass

Reading Comprehension

DIRECTIONS ▶

Read each passage. Then read each question about the passage. Decide which is the best answer to the question. Mark the space for the answer you have chosen.

SAMPLES

The Harvest Moon

The harvest moon is the full moon that occurs each year closest to the first day of autumn. For centuries people have thought that this moon looked bigger and brighter than any other moon, and for centuries people have held celebrations to honor it. The harvest moon is not really bigger or brighter than any other moon, but it looks like it is because it is closer to the horizon. At this time of year the moon travels on its lowest path. For several days in a row, it appears close to the horizon just as the sun sets. On clear autumn nights the moon glows brilliantly. Some people think it looks orange.

In agricultural communities long ago, farmers took advantage of the bright light of this autumn moon to harvest their crops. Many people in these communities believed that the harvest moon appeared in the sky to signal the end of the harvest. Many others believed it appeared to grant them successful crops. People all over the world held lavish festivals under the harvest moon. China, for example, still holds a harvest moon festival. The celebration in China involves telling stories of Heng O, a figure in Chinese myths who controlled the fruitfulness of the harvest. The people of China honor the moon by baking round cakes and stamping them with an image of Heng O. Then they take these cakes to the festival and exchange them with friends and relatives to wish them happiness and luck with the next year's crops.

A

The harvest moon festival in China is *mainly* a celebration of —

A the holidays

B the harvest

C Heng O

D the full moon

B

Which of the following is true of the autumn moon?

A It grants successful crops.

B It houses Heng O.

C It controls the earth's fruitfulness.

D It travels near the horizon.

Harvest Moon

Drowsy after a day of carnival fun,

Rocked gently homeward in the car,

I have almost fallen asleep

when the moon rises like a dream

5 outside my back-seat window.

It is the world's largest Ferris wheel,

bright as a beacon,

welcoming all riders.

It is a giant pumpkin slowly ripening,

10 outgrowing its protective ground cover.

It is the face of a smiling friend

who wants to play hide-and-seek

behind the highway's bare trees.

I smile back at my friend

15 and drift off to sleep.

Maybe I'll play when I awaken.

1

What has caused the speaker to be tired?

A A day at the carnival

B The car's highway motion

C Moonlight in the speaker's face

D A game of hide-and-seek

2

What is the main idea of this poem?

A The carnival is a lot of fun.

B Moonlight creates a peaceful atmosphere.

C Somebody else should drive when you're sleepy.

D You should spend quality time with your friends.

3

The moon is compared to a Ferris wheel, a pumpkin, and a friend's face. What type of literary device is this?

A Allusion   **C** Metaphor

B Apostrophe   **D** Simile

4

What is causing the moon to "play hide-and-seek"?

A It has sunk below the horizon.

B It is in its new, or dark, phase.

C Cloud movement is obscuring it.

D The car's movement is obscuring it.

5

How does the speaker feel about the moon?

A Afraid   **C** Excited

B Bored   **D** Affectionate

6

The moon is compared to a pumpkin and to a friend's face. What effect does this have on the poem?

A It recounts the day's happy events.

B It connects the images to happy and seasonal events.

C It tells a story from the moon's point of view.

D It highlights the eerie descriptions in the poem.

If No One Sees a Sport, Does It Make a Sound?

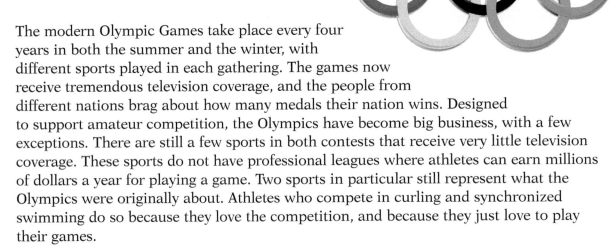

The modern Olympic Games take place every four years in both the summer and the winter, with different sports played in each gathering. The games now receive tremendous television coverage, and the people from different nations brag about how many medals their nation wins. Designed to support amateur competition, the Olympics have become big business, with a few exceptions. There are still a few sports in both contests that receive very little television coverage. These sports do not have professional leagues where athletes can earn millions of dollars a year for playing a game. Two sports in particular still represent what the Olympics were originally about. Athletes who compete in curling and synchronized swimming do so because they love the competition, and because they just love to play their games.

The Olympic Summer Games has basketball, track and field, and gymnastics, among others. These are sports that most people know about. Synchronized swimming does not get the same attention as the sports mentioned, but it may be the most physically difficult sport of all. Like gymnasts, synchronized swimmers have to perform flips, spins, turns, and other moves set to music. Unlike gymnasts, the eight synchronized swimmers on a team have to perform all of their moves at the exact same time, and they have to do half of those moves underwater. Many synchronized swimming moves involve the swimmers kicking their legs into the air while their heads are underwater. Swimmers are judged on style, length of time under the water, and on how high their bodies push out of the water on a move. By the way, the entire routine, which lasts five minutes, takes place in a pool where the swimmers cannot touch the bottom.

In the Winter Olympics, nearly everyone has heard of hockey, skiing, and speed skating. How many people have heard of the sport of curling? This sport was developed almost 600 years ago in Scotland when people couldn't play golf. Curling is played on the ice with actual stones weighing almost forty pounds each. On opposite ends of the ice are two areas enclosed by circles. Players on each team take turns sliding their stones across the ice, trying to get them as close to the center circle as possible. During a stone's trip across the ice, players on the team use brooms to sweep the ice in front of the moving stone. This smoothes out the ice and makes the stones go farther.

Curlers and synchronized swimmers love to play their sports, whether anyone is watching on television or not. Their goal is to be the best in the world, and a price cannot be put on that.

7

The main idea of the passage is —

A that curlers and swimmers really love their sports

B that the Olympic Games are not fair to curling and swimming

C that curling and swimming are easier to play than other sports

D that winter Olympic sports are harder than summer Olympic sports

8

What question could be asked to determine how long swimmers must stay underwater?

A How many moves make up a routine?

B How fast can swimmers move?

C How many minutes give a high score?

D How many minutes underwater gets a high score?

9

Which of these *best* describes the structure of this passage?

A Story used to give a lesson

B Question and answer by paragraph

C Facts and opinions given to persuade

D General information, then specific information

10

Which statement is generally true of the Olympics?

A The games usually take place indoors.

B Most nations win at least one medal.

C Some athletes do not get paid to play their sport.

D The summer and winter games are in the same place.

11

What information is needed in the passage to explain how synchronized swimming is won?

A The time for a routine

B The number of judges

C The scoring system used

D The number of swimmers

12

Why do curlers sweep the ice in front of a moving stone?

A To make the stone go faster

B To make the stone go farther

C To keep the stone on target

D To keep the stone from sliding

You're Invited!
It's a Treasure Hunt!

Come to Sarah Sanchez's birthday party and search for hidden treasure. Be the first team to find all the clues and win the treasure!

Where: Springfield Botanical Gardens and Living History Farm

When: Saturday, October 22; 2:00 P.M.–4:00 P.M.

What to Wear: Old clothes and boots or hiking shoes

Please Reply: 555-0102

Ground Rules:

Teams of three or four will be given treasure maps, notebooks, and twelve mystery clues. Each team will try to hunt down all twelve mystery clues and return to base camp to claim the treasure.

Sample Clues:

What's the nickname of the Living History Farm's dairy cow?

How many different kinds of roses grow in the Faulkner Rose Garden?

How does the "Seed Spotter" work in the Gardens' gift shop?

Directions:

to Springfield Botanical Gardens and Living History Farm
From Interstate 10 (going north)
Exit at Plank Rd. West.
Follow Plank Rd. west for about two miles to Silverton Ave.
Turn north (right) on Silverton Ave.
Follow Silverton Avenue about 1 mile to Jordan Farm Rd.
Turn west (left) on Jordan Farm Rd.
Follow Jordan Farm Rd. to Botanical Gardens entrance (about 1 mile).

13

Which words *best* tell what guests will be doing at the party?

A "old clothes, boots, or hiking shoes"

B "turn north (right) on Silverton Ave."

C "each team will try to hunt down all twelve mystery clues"

D "Springfield Botanical Gardens and Living History Farm"

14

Which of the following is *probably* true about the treasure hunt?

A Each team will look for a different set of clues.

B Guests will get to pick which team they are on.

C Sarah Sanchez will be on the first team to be formed.

D All teams will start the treasure hunt at about the same time.

15

Friends of Sarah would *probably* —

A skim the invitation

B take notes on the invitation

C read the invitation carefully

D scan the invitation for their names

16

Sarah has invited friends who *probably* —

A do not like to compete

B prefer indoor activities

C enjoy outdoor adventures

D have been on treasure hunts before

17

Which of the following is *most* true about the invitation?

A It is persuasive.

B It is descriptive.

C It appeals to the senses.

D It provides basic information.

18

The *most likely* thing to spoil the party would be that —

A the weather is terrible

B Sarah's best friend doesn't attend

C Sarah's friends don't know one another

D the gardens and farm are closed Sunday

School Day 2200

Anna was having a really great dream when her alarm went off. She tried to stay asleep, but that's hard to do when your bed is tilting upward to place you on your feet.

"Mom," she called, "my bed is set too early!"

Anna's mother breezed into the room and checked the setting. "No, it's seven on the dot. Rise and shine!"

Anna groaned and kicked away her covers. She sleepily turned on the cleaning field and stepped through it. Waves of invisible energy left her skin clean and fresh. She set the clothes-maker on "autumn casual" and watched her outfit take shape. She was waiting for the finishing touches when her mom called, "Hurry up, Anna; you'll miss the shuttle!"

"I'm coming!" she retorted.

In the kitchen Anna said, "I don't know why you can't fly me to school, Mom. Rachel's mom does."

"Rachel's mom hasn't chosen an employment shift yet. Now, eat your breakfast."

As Anna ate, her mother held a scanner above her forehead. "Good grief, Anna! You're low on half of your vitamin levels. What have you been having for lunch? I'm going to make you a nice—"

"No time, Mom," said Anna, as she dashed for the transport tube. "I have to catch the shuttle, remember?"

The shuttle *accelerated* into orbit, with the same boring view of Earth outside the windows. Anna's friends George and Chan got into trouble as usual, launching paper missiles across the weightless cabin and then pretending they hadn't. Finally, Mr. Dennis bellowed, "No horseplay, boys!"

After the shuttle docked, the kids floated down the hallways to their classes. In history that day, Anna learned about kids in the twenty-first century. They didn't go to school in space stations; they walked or rode to schools on the ground. There were no transport tubes, either; people used cars to get around. Kids had to shop for clothes because houses didn't come with clothes-makers. Their parents had to go find jobs rather than choose an employment shift. It was all very difficult to imagine.

That evening Anna's mother asked, "How was school, dear?" She always asked this, and Anna usually just said "Fine," but tonight she felt like talking.

"We learned about the twenty-first century," Anna said, remembering all the strange things her teaching screen had shown her.

"That sounds interesting."

"It was," said Anna. "Kids were really different creatures back then."

19

Based on the passage, what is the best definition for the word *accelerated*?

A Slowed down   **C** Turned left

B Sped up   **D** Turned right

20

Which detail *best* supports the idea that Anna's world is different from today's?

A Her alarm goes off too early on school days.

B Her friends sometimes get into trouble.

C Her mother worries about her eating habits.

D Her school bus is a space shuttle.

21

Which idea from the passage *best* contrasts the fact that Anna attends school on a space station?

A People had to shop for clothes.

B People used cars to get around.

C Kids walked or rode to school.

D Kids went to schools on the ground.

22

This passage is an example of —

A fiction   **C** drama

B monologue   **D** poetry

23

Which detail is *most* important to the main idea of the passage?

A Anna's bed is also an alarm clock.

B Anna's understanding of the twenty-first century is limited.

C Anna's interest in the world around her is limited.

D Anna's teacher is a computer screen.

24

Why is it inaccurate for Anna to say, "Kids were really different creatures back then"?

A She hasn't finished studying the lesson on the twenty-first century.

B She hasn't learned how society functioned in the twenty-first century.

C She doesn't realize that kids act similarly in both time periods.

D She doesn't realize that parents act similarly in both time periods.

In a Galaxy Far, Far Away

When looking up at a clear night sky, most people would say that the stars seem to twinkle. In reality, the light from the stars is not blinking brighter and dimmer. Instead, Earth's atmosphere changes the way we see the light from those stars. The gases in the atmosphere cause the light from distant stars to bend, sometimes even back upon itself. The atmosphere is what makes the stars appear to twinkle. It is also what makes it difficult to see things very far away, even with the most powerful telescope.

What about building a telescope that reaches above Earth's atmosphere? It would be impossible to build a telescope over 100 miles tall, but could you build a large telescope and then put it into orbit? The answer, of course, is yes. The Hubble Telescope, launched in 1990, orbits Earth at 380 miles above its surface. It takes pictures of the planets in our solar system, as well as stars in distant galaxies. In fact, the telescope is named for the astronomer who discovered that there were galaxies in space other than our own Milky Way galaxy. Unfortunately, Edwin P. Hubble, who died in 1953, never got to see the telescope that bears his name.

Edwin Powell Hubble was born in Marshfield, Missouri, in 1889. He thought he would be a lawyer when he grew up. However, he changed his mind soon after he began studying law at Oxford University in 1910. He later said that, even if he would not be as gifted an astronomer as he would be a lawyer, astronomy was more important and so it was where he should spend his time. It turned out that he made the right choice.

Hubble received his Ph.D. in astronomy in 1917. Two years later, he became a member of the staff at the Mount Wilson Observatory outside of Pasadena, California. Mount Wilson was home to one of the largest telescopes in the world at that time. It measures more than 8 feet in diameter at its base. Hubble used this telescope to see something astronomers called the Andromeda Nebula. Hubble used his calculations to show that Andromeda was actually another galaxy. Hubble soon proved that there were other galaxies even farther away than Andromeda, and that these galaxies were moving away. In 1929, he showed that the farther away a galaxy is from Earth, the faster it is moving away from the Milky Way. This became known as Hubble's Law. Instead of studying the law, then, Hubble actually made one.

25

What is the name of the galaxy that contains Earth?

A Andromeda   **C** Milky Way

B Marshfield   **D** Nebula

26

Which sentence supports the conclusion that objects in space look blurry when seen through a ground telescope?

A The light from objects in space makes them twinkle.

B Objects in space are moving quickly away from Earth.

C Objects in space are billions of miles away from Earth.

D The atmosphere interferes with light from objects in space.

27

This biographical passage is unusual because it begins by describing —

A where the subject was born

B where the subject went to school

C something named after the subject

D something of interest to the subject

28

Which demonstrates that the author admires Edwin Hubble?

A The author seems happy that he will follow in Hubble's footsteps.

B The author seems pleased that Hubble gave up his study of law.

C The author seems interested in the telescope that Hubble designed.

D The author seems sad that Hubble never saw the Hubble Telescope.

29

The title of this passage encourages the reader to read for —

A the origin of the universe

B what makes a powerful telescope

C space objects within the Milky Way

D information on distant space objects

30

The passage explains all of the following *except* —

A why Hubble's Law is important

B the height of the Hubble Telescope

C the speed of the Andromeda galaxy

D why Edwin Hubble became an astronomer

Use Your Head—Wear a Helmet

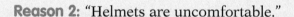

Everyone should wear a helmet when he or she rides a bike. Professional bike racers wear helmets. You should too.

Many people say they don't wear a helmet — for some very weak reasons.

Reason 1: "I've never worn a helmet and nothing has happened to me so far."

Fact: Bike crashes can happen anywhere, at any time. Studies show that three out of four bike crashes result in a head injury. Even professional bike racers can crash.

Reason 2: "Helmets are uncomfortable."

Fact: New helmet designs have made helmets stronger yet lighter and more comfortable than ever before. Look for the safety sticker inside (CPSC, ASTM, or Snell B-95) that shows that the helmet meets government and Consumer Product Safety Commission standards.

Reason 3: "Helmets aren't cool."

Fact: Helmets are designed to help prevent skull and brain injuries. A serious crash can cause brain damage or death, which is definitely not cool.

Reason 4: "I'm afraid I'll stand out too much."

Fact: That's the point! You want your clothing, including your helmet, to help motorists, other bikers, and pedestrians see you. That way they'll be less likely to run into you.

SAFETY TIP
Make sure your helmet fits securely and covers the top, sides, and back of your head. If your forehead is exposed, your helmet won't protect you in a crash.

31

An experienced bike rider looking for information on helmet safety stickers *probably* would —

A read the poster carefully

B scan the poster for this information

C skim the poster to make a summary

D assume the poster contained no related information

32

The "Safety Tip" will lead most readers to conclude that —

A people have to be persuaded to buy a good-quality helmet

B bicycle helmets fall off during crashes

C an ill-fitting helmet may not be adequate protection in a crash

D bicycle helmets fit better than other types of helmets

33

Which of the following is a fact?

A Most helmets are unattractive.

B Many helmets are uncomfortable.

C Many bike crashes ruin friendships.

D Most bike crashes result in head injuries.

34

Most people reading this poster will *probably* —

A buy a new helmet

B consider riding their bikes less often

C assume the facts are based on evidence

D research Consumer Product Safety Commission standards

35

The creators of this poster are urging readers to —

A become lifelong bicycle enthusiasts

B encourage friends to buy new helmets

C consider riding bikes to work or school

D think about safety before personal appearance

36

Someone reading this poster could *probably* assume that —

A helmet designs are about to change

B dark-colored clothing is safest

C safety standards have improved helmet design

D wearing a helmet might soon become the law

Sticking to It

Kenny and I stood nervously before the desk of Ralph, our boss. My stomach felt like I had swallowed a bag of rocks.

"Gentlemen," Ralph said softly, "what did I tell you yesterday?"

We fidgeted for a moment, and then Kenny answered. "You said if we didn't finish pulling those weeds by the end of the day, we'd be out of a job."

"And did you?"

After another pause, Kenny said, "No."

"Then I guess you'd better go on home," said Ralph.

Kenny left, and I was about to follow when Ralph held up one hand. I stopped and waited for him to speak.

I thought back on my job. It was my second year working on the public golf course. While many of my friends were lounging around all summer, I was getting to work at 6:45 A.M. and laying sod, mowing, and watering into the evening. The work was hard and hot, but I enjoyed it.

The "green," the grass around a golf hole, is as short and smooth as living-room carpet—or is supposed to be, anyway. The grass around hole sixteen was infested with crabgrass, which made the surface bumpy. We had to get down on our hands and knees and cut it out piece by piece with short, sharp blades.

We cut and we cut, but the grass seemed to grow back even faster. Kenny started making frequent trips to the water fountain—even when we'd just been there. He took long breaks in the nearby shade. It was hard to be the only one doing any work, so I slowed down, too. Then one day Ralph drove up, a scowl on his face, and I realized he'd been watching us all along.

Suddenly Ralph spoke. "Kenny isn't a very good worker," he finally said, "but I know you are—or were. So I will give you a choice."

I thought about the endless crabgrass. I thought about my friends lounging around. I thought about how it felt to be considered a bad worker.

"I'll stick to it," I said.

"Here's your clippers," he replied.

By that afternoon I had cleaned out a surprisingly large section of the green. Hearing a truck door slam, I looked up to see Ralph studying my work, clippers in hand.

"Good job," he said. "I knew you had it in you." Then he bent down and joined me.

37

How does the speaker feel about almost losing his job?

A Confused   **C** Relieved

B Excited   **D** Upset

38

Why does the speaker almost lose his job?

A He begins sneaking over to a swimming pool.

B He has forgotten how to do the work.

C The golf course no longer needs him.

D The quality of his work has dropped off.

39

Why does the speaker decide to stay on the job?

A He doesn't want to be considered a bad worker.

B He doesn't want to disappoint his family.

C He likes the job.

D He needs the money.

40

Which of the following was *not* a reason why Kenny lost his job?

A He came in late for work.

B He left his partner to work alone.

C He took long breaks in the shade.

D He took too many water breaks.

41

Why does Ralph help the speaker at the end of the passage?

A He doesn't want the speaker to quit.

B He is pleased with the speaker's work.

C He is testing a new crabgrass tool.

D He needs the green ready for tournament play.

42

Which of the following *best* summarizes the main theme of this passage?

A Idle hands make mischief.

B Let your work speak highly of you.

C Make new friends but keep the old.

D You are known by the company you keep.

Gigantic Trees

Have you ever read about an automobile running into a large tree? What if the tree were hollow? And what if that hollow tree were so wide that a car could pass right through its trunk without doing any damage to the tree or itself? Well, if that car happened to be driving through Sequoia National Forest in Northern California, that could almost happen. Sequoia trees are the largest trees in the world, and they grow almost exclusively near the northern coast of California and the Sierra Mountains.

What is the difference between giant sequoias and redwoods? Both giant sequoias and redwoods belong to the same tree family, but the name *sequoia* comes from Sequoyah, the famous Cherokee. It is not the scientific name for the tree family, but it is the name everyone uses. Both sequoias and redwoods are some of the largest trees in the world. They both stay green year-round. The main difference is that the giant sequoias are shorter than redwoods, while the trunks of giant sequoias are larger in diameter.

Just how big can redwoods and giant sequoias get? Redwoods are the tallest known trees in the world. The tallest of these giants stands 368 feet tall, taller than most office buildings. Its lowest branches are 150 feet from the ground. Luckily, its cones are only an inch long and very light. If they were heavier, they could hurt someone when they fell from 150 feet in the air. The largest giant sequoia has a name —General Sherman Tree. It stretches *only* 275 feet into the air, but its trunk is more than 30 feet wide. If General Sherman Tree were hollowed out, you could drive a tank through its trunk without touching the sides!

Are these trees very old? The trees in the sequoia family are some of the oldest living things on this planet. Scientists estimate that General Sherman Tree could be 2,500 years old. This estimated age is based on counting the rings of another giant sequoia that was cut down before a law was passed protecting the trees. When scientists counted the growth rings inside that tree, they found that it was alive in 1305 B.C. These huge trees are extremely resistant to disease. Now that sequoias are protected, there is no reason to think General Sherman Tree and others will not continue to live for another 2,500 years.

43

What is unusual about sequoia leaves?

A They are hollow.

B They are very small.

C They stay green all year.

D They are shaped like cones.

44

How do scientists determine the age of a sequoia?

A By counting the rings inside the trunk

B By counting the number of yellow leaves

C By measuring the length of a piece of bark

D By measuring the height of the tallest branch

45

The structure of this passage can be defined as —

A facts and opinions

B questions and answers

C theories and conclusions

D main idea and supporting details

46

Which of these pieces of information is in the text?

A The age of the oldest redwood

B The location of General Sherman Tree

C The name of the tallest tree in the world

D The importance of Sequoyah, the Cherokee

47

Which of these supports the idea that General Sherman Tree will live a long time?

A Sequoias rarely get diseases.

B Sequoias keep their leaves year-round.

C Scientists have counted its rings.

D Scientists have measured its trunk.

48

From the information about sequoias, it is clear that they —

A can become hollow

B are taller than redwoods

C are used for lumber in California

D need to live near the ocean

Composting for the Future

Don't Throw It Away. Reuse It!

Composting is nature's way of recycling. Most of what we eat and what we cut, trim, and rake in our yards can be added to a compost heap. Composting returns vital ingredients to the soil. So don't throw nature's products away. Reuse them!

It's Easy to Compost!

Follow these simple steps and you'll soon enjoy the benefits of composting for the future.

1 Place yard trimmings and food scraps in a pile or bin outside.

2 As the older trimmings age, mix newer "greener" trimmings with them.

3 After 12 to 16 months, the material at the bottom of the heap should have "composted" into rich, sweet-smelling soil.

4 Add this compost to flower beds or lawns, or spread it around the base of trees and bushes. Using compost saves water and provides your plants with good food.

Join the Club!

When you start composting, you'll be joining Mayor Shelton and city council members in recycling the best of Springfield!

Food scraps including fruits, vegetables, tea leaves, and coffee grounds are okay. Do not compost meat, fish, poultry, bones, sauces, dairy products, fats, oils, or pet waste.

49

Many residents of Springfield probably —

A support the mayor's efforts

B own houses with yards

C believe in recycling newspapers

D spend more time outdoors than indoors

50

The directions for composting are —

A brief and factual

B highly descriptive

C difficult to follow

D highly persuasive

51

Which of the following is *not* discussed in the city's flyer?

A Why composting saves water

B Whether raked leaves can be composted

C How long material should be left in the compost pile

D What kinds of food scraps should not be composted

52

The main, *unstated* reason that Springfield wants its citizens to compost is probably that —

A the mayor thinks it is a good idea

B composting has become popular

C composting returns vital ingredients to the soil

D the city wants to reduce the amount of garbage it hauls

53

Based on this flyer, one can assume that composting is —

A a tradition in Springfield

B a way to meet one's neighbors

C an inexpensive alternative to using fertilizer

D another way of disposing of bottles

54

The city might use the same ideas behind the composting campaign to urge citizens to —

A take fewer vacations out of state

B donate toys and clothing to charity

C use oil lamps instead of electricity

D plant more flowers in their yards